Get Competitive!
Cut Costs and
Improve Quality

Lynn Tylczak

Illustrations by Edith Harrison

LIBERTY HALL
PRESS™

LIBERTY HALL PRESS books are published by LIBERTY HALL PRESS, an imprint of TAB BOOKS. TAB BOOKS is a division of McGraw-Hill, Inc. Its trademark, consisting of the words "LIBERTY HOUSE" and the portrayal of Benjamin Franklin, is registered in the United States Patent and Trademark Office.

First Edition
First Printing

©1990 by LIBERTY HALL PRESS, an imprint of TAB BOOKS
TAB BOOKS is a division of McGraw-Hill, Inc.

Library of Congress Cataloging-in-Publication Data

Tylczak, Lynn.
   Get competitive! : cut costs and improve quality / by Lynn
Tylczak.
      p. cm.
   Includes bibliographical references.
   ISBN 0-8306-8476-X :
   1. Cost control. 2. Quality control. 3. Industrial productivity.
4. Competition, International. I. Title.
HD47.3.T95 1990   90-5708
658.15′52—dc20   CIP

TAB BOOKS offers software for sale.
For information and a catalog, please contact:
TAB Software Department
Blue Ridge Summit, PA 17294-0850

Questions regarding the content of this book
should be addressed to:
Reader Inquiry Branch
TAB BOOKS
Blue Ridge Summit, PA 17294-0214

Vice President & Editorial Director: David Conti
Book Editor: Roman Gorski
Production: Katherine G. Brown
Book Design: Jaclyn J. Boone
Cover Design: Lori E. Schlosser

Contents

Acknowledgments

With greatest appreciation to Art Mudge, CVS, author
and authority;
the Bureau of Business Practice;
Value Digest;
the dozens of business leaders who were willing to share their
competitive successes;
and—last but not least—Erik, Lesley, and Joseph Tylczak.

Preface

"Never ask a barber if you need a haircut, a salesman if his is a good price, or a Value Manager if VM will work on a given project," says Theresa Barlow, President of Barlow and Associates, Quincy, IL. "The answer to the former is 'yes,' the answer to the latter is 'yes,' and the third answer is an average of the two. But any Value Manager will tell you that while VM works on all types of projects, it's not equally or economically suited to all applications."

According to John Maurer of Westinghouse's Productivity and Quality Center, "In the not so good old days, companies developed products/services in a series. A design would go to engineering, then to drafting, then to manufacturing, then to marketing, etc. It worked something like a relay race. Every department ran its lap with the product, then passed it off to the next in line. After each pass of the baton, the product was a little more locked in. The people further down the line had less of a chance to add their valuable input. Last but not least, the product would end up in the sales department, where the sales team would have only one role to play in the product's evolution: the 'creationism' of sales. That used to work (although 'how well' might be debatable) but it won't work any more. In today's competitive environment, products need to meet the test of the market, as well as the test of the internal corporate decision machine. VM utilizes an interactive and multidiscipline team that simultaneously considers sales, marketing, design, manufacturing, etc., issues. The only way to develop a product that competes on all levels is to see that all levels are addressed in initial product development. That means VM is the most effective, level-headed approach.''

According to Bob Mitchell, CVS, there are three types of businesses. ''Some use the 'ready, fire, aim' approach. No good. Others use 'ready, aim, aim, aim, aim . . . .' Not much better. VM thinkers don't act instead of think or think instead of act. They think BEFORE they act.''

Theresa Barlow repeats an intriguing tale: ''The VM team at a large midwest manufacturer asked 'Who manufactures Component A at our competitor's factory?' Company machinists hated the boring and time-consuming work involved in the component, and turnover in the department was high. Researchers learned that the competition had simplified the production process so that lower paid, virtually unskilled laborers could handle it. When the subject company modified its production process, it realized 30% cost savings, higher component quality, and a lower turnover of machinists, who were able to use their skills in more challenging and interesting work. The company cut its prices and sales soared.'' That's VM—news you'll use.

Introduction

Our national economy is approaching its final day of "wreckoning."

The problem can be summarized in five words: competitive— *they* are, *we* aren't. Fewer and fewer products are made in the U.S.A., and many of *those* are having trouble maintaining (let alone increasing) their market share against cheaper and/or higher quality foreign goods. Even a car proudly advertised as "Born in America" needs numerous organ transplants from abroad to be competitive.

According to a 1987 *U.S. News and World Report* poll, nine out of 10 Americans worry that we are losing our competitive edge. They aren't alone. The magazine also reported that business executives worldwide rated the U.S. as only the fifth most competitive nation (top honors, of course, went to Japan and West Germany).

From political parties to the commercial community, competitive rhetoric runs rampant, but wispy words don't do the problem justice. It takes firm facts to solidify the scene. Such facts are to current rhetoric what bullets are to an empty gun.

THE PROBLEM WITH PRODUCTIVITY

The game of Increased Productivity (which allows businesses to cut prices and/or raise wages and/or increase profits) is no "Trivial Pursuit," yet our foreign competitors seem to have a "Monopoly" on it. For example, it takes 80 to 100 hours for the Japanese to build a car; American companies need 150 to 160. Between 1981 and 1985, our growth in output per worker was 1/6 that of Korea and 1/3 that of Japan. Our rank growth in productivity ranks 11th among the 12 developed nations.

A QUESTION OF QUALITY

Our workers not only produce less, they produce "lesser." Westinghouse used to sample product quality at the end of a production line. In 1979, the company decided to copy the Japanese and check "composite yield" (the amount of work each employee did correctly the first time) and found that extensive reworking and after-the-fact fixing slashed quality in some plants to as low as 15%.

When Harvard Business School Professor David Garvin studied Japanese manufacturers of air-conditioners, he found fewer assembly-line defects and service calls, a higher output per man-hour, and lower overall quality costs than are documented in their American counterparts. According to a study by TRW, American cars average 3.5 repairs a year; Japanese cars require only 1.1.

THE CRISIS OF COST/PROFITABILITY

Americans produce less and less, but at a higher cost and lower profit. Since 1980, the pretax rate of return on U.S. manufacturing assets has steadily declined. In one year alone, it dove by almost 10%. In some industries, the outlook is particularly bad. According to Seymour Fabric of the Southern California Shoe Manufacturers Association, the domestic industry is "doomed," and he isn't spinning yarns. The industry is labor-intensive. In Brazil, workers earn 85 cents per hour, while U.S. workers earn an average of $6.71. No wonder foreign competitors are a shoe-in for the market.

THE DISASTROUS DEFICIT

In 1974, our economy got off track and has since become intractable. The U.S. (which had a trade surplus in 1979) is now the world's biggest debtor. In six years, our trade deficit with South Korea, Taiwan, Singapore, and Hong Kong rose *2,900%*. In 10 years, our Japanese shortfall rose from $1.6 billion to $40.7 billion.

In 1980, the U.S. had a trade surplus in high-tech goods of $26 billion, by 1986, we had a deficit of $2.5 billion, a seven-year decline of 489%.

UNFAIR COMPETITION

Countries are not created equal. Each has unique strengths and politically-propped weaknesses. Storm clouds are gathering on the U.S. business horizon, and unfair competition is one "hail" of an example.

Some governments only buy from the home team, no matter how foul its batting average. Some subsidize (Japan gave Turkey a 25-year, $205-million loan at 5% interest to finance a Japanese-built bridge across the Bosporus Strait). Quotas foil foreign footholds (Italy limits Japanese auto imports to 2,200 units annually, less than 1% of its market). Duties are dutifully imposed (the U.S. sticks to a 6.5% duty on Korean bicycles, while Korea's 100% duty really sticks it to our bicycle builders).

Silly standards are yet another "stop imports" strategy. The Japanese government compiled a "master" list of approved preservatives and colorants for use in cosmetics and grooming aids. Fine. However, it *also* developed a supplemental list of acceptable additives—and *that* list is only available to Japanese manufacturers! The beauty business is skin-deep, and the Japanese have a very thin skin.

This type of unfair competition raises some questions. If foreign countries are playing dirty, why should we stay lily-white (or, at least, off-white)? Why not protect our own markets? There are two good reasons: protectionism would cost us money, and protectionism simply wouldn't work.

Protecting U.S. shoemakers would be expensive ($26,300 a year to save each $14,000 job). Within a year, shoe prices would climb by 15%. Worse, shooing imports away would hurt Brazil, a country that needs the foreign exchange to pay its debts to U.S. banks. We would be robbing Peter to pay protected Paul.

We know the down side of protectionism. The Tariff Act of 1930 prompted 25 of our major trading partners to retaliate with sanctions of their own. The stock market lost ground for two years while exports fell by two-thirds. If protectionism still sounds good, it's because you're not listening.

The key point is that *we can't legislate away the basic strengths of our trading partners*. The Japanese have a very strong work ethic. The average American works 1,836 hours per year, whereas the average Japanese works 2,116 (an additional two months for no additional pay). The Japanese forego over 60% of their vacation time. Their work ethic may be a thorn in our economic side, but we can't force them to stop and smell the roses.

Japanese companies can get low-cost capital. In Japan, interest rates are low and savings rates are high. The Japanese save 18% of their take-home pay; we barely save 6%.

Our lack of competitiveness must be a call to action, not a call to hasty reaction. Protectionism is a band-aid approach to massive economic trauma. *We need to attack the heart of our competitive problem: high product prices and low product quality.*

A NOTE TO SMALL BUSINESS OWNERS

It doesn't matter if your major competitor is across the ocean or across the street. You may be fighting Japan, Inc. or just trying to keep up with The Jones, Ltd. Either way, if you can cut costs and/or increase quality, you can improve your bottom line.

Dozens of top companies have done just that. A little-known technique called Value Management (VM) has a 40-year history of cutting costs and improving quality for such companies as Rockwell, Texas Instruments, Westinghouse, Xerox, Boeing, GE, Hughes Aircraft, TRW, Du Pont, and GM. Does this corporate list sound familiar? Read (or review) *In Search of Excellence*. Don't bother looking for VM in the index—it isn't there. For VM, *this* is the book to read.

VM works for these winners as it has worked for hundreds of other, smaller companies. Odds are, it will work for you, too. It can help you get—dare we say it?—more competitive.

1

The Whole Story

THE MAJOR ADVANTAGE OF FAIRY TALES IS THAT THEY TELL the whole story, start ("Once upon a time" . . .) to finish (". . . and they all lived happily ever after.") No nagging loose ends to keep us at loose ends (e.g., but soon, Cinderella realized that being a princess wasn't enough—she wanted a meaningful job as well).

Welcome to the real world where business magazines tell us *what* successful companies have accomplished, but not *how*. It's like ending a suspenseful, no-way-out short story with the cliche, ". . . and then he woke up." We feel cheated. We want to know success-building secrets *so that we can copy them*.

A major business magazine recently ran three corporate success stories without explaining how success was attained. This is the mystery genre's equivalent of ". . . and the murderer is—THE END." The theme of this special report was competition. After a half-dozen deflating pages ("Can America Compete?"), the magazine trotted out three corporate thoroughbreds that buck the negative trend. The first was General Electric, which spent $11.6 billion to boost its competitiveness (e.g., its simplified locomotive door now requires 40% fewer parts and costs 25 to 30% less). The second was Black & Decker, which multiplied sales sixfold while cutting prices in half. Third was Westinghouse with its 300-person Productivity and Quality Center (1986 income up 50% over 1983, sales up by 13%, etc.).

What the magazine *didn't* tell us is that General Electric, Black & Decker, and Westinghouse used VM to achieve these impressive results. A GE employee first developed Value Management (a.k.a. Value Engineering/Analysis) in 1957, and the company has been a prime practitioner ever since. The company's major appliance division used VM to:

- Reduce the manual handling of tubs and doorliners by 85%.
- Reduce the number of factory parts and assemblies from 5,600 to 850.
- Slash the product manufacturing cycle from between five and six days to 18 hours.
- Reduce service rates by more than one-third.
- Double the inventory turns of both raw and in-progress goods, etc. (Fig. 1-1).

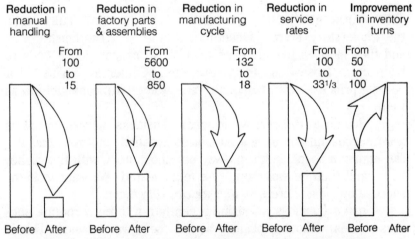

Fig. 1-1. General Electric's impressive results after incorporating VM.

Black & Decker utilizes VM to decrease the number of parts in its professional hand tools, to increase manufacturing productivity, and to improve product reliability. B&D's ongoing VM program more than justifies its costs. One-time VM studies average a 15-to-1 return on investment, ongoing programs average 25-to-1 or better.

Westinghouse was a VM leader even before it opened its Productivity and Quality Center (which, incidentally, provides VM assistance to the company's far-flung facilities). Thanks to a value study conducted on the Advanced Energy Systems Division's proprietary photovoltaic device:

- The number of steps in the manufacturing process was cut from 14 to 10.
- Quality in terms of yield was increased by 13%.
- The number of handling operations was reduced by 83%.
- The number of people required to operate the plant was reduced by 37%.
- Westinghouse now receives greater product output for 18% lower manufacturing costs while having increased product quality (Fig. 1-2).

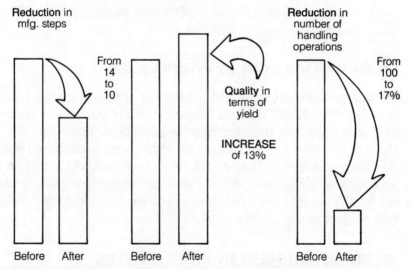

Fig. 1-2. Westinghouse receives greater product output for 18% lower costs while having increased quality.

VM has a phenomenal track record, but has never been on the fast track for publicity. Value practitioners keep it something of a secret. "Why tell our competitors how to improve product quality and cut costs by 30%?" asks Bob Gaylor, a value specialist at Freightliner.

Still, the little-known technique's track record speaks for itself. VM can cut costs while improving quality in virtually any department (purchasing, manufacturing, administration, capital construction, etc.) of virtually any business (large or small) in any industry (manufacturing or service).

VALUE MANAGEMENT BY DEPARTMENT

- Purchasing: Using VM, Joy Manufacturing (Pittsburgh, PA) cut the cost of a special 1/4-20 brass jam nut from $13.30 per hundred to $6.30.

- Manufacturing: By VMing components, Ansul (Marinette, WI) cut the wholesale cost of its fire extinguisher from $15.20 to $11.75.

- Administration: According to Jack F. Reichert, President and CEO, the Brunswick Corporation used VM to save about $18 million in annual overhead.

- Capital construction: VM is probably best-known for its ability to save 40 to 60% on construction projects. In Heppner, Oregon, a $40,000 VM study saved project owners $11.6 million (a whopping 290-to-1 ROI).

VALUE MANAGEMENT BY COMPANY SIZE

Many large companies use VM. About half of the companies listed in *In Search of Excellence* have adopted it. Many smaller companies have also used it to their competitive advantage. Weiss-Aug (Parsippany, NJ) used VM to cut the cost of its phone hook switch from 50 cents to 31 cents. At Kistler-Morse (Redmond, WA), VM on a solid-state strain gauge cut costs (the cost of one component was cut by 400%), improved delivery schedules, and provided consistent product quality. And so it goes.

VALUE MANAGEMENT BY INDUSTRY TYPE

VM has been successfully used to manufacture everything from product-packaging systems (St. Regis, Du Pont) to truck cabs (Mack Truck, Freightliner) to consumer products (West Bend, Duncan) to energy conservation systems (PPG Industries, Pittsburgh Corning Corporation).

VM is relatively new to service industries, but what its track record lacks in depth it makes up for in cold hard facts. The 98-member hospital council of Western Pennsylvania found that, collectively, the facilities could save almost $3.5 million a year by revising their standard admissions kit. VM determined that only six of the 57 personal care items included in the kit were routinely required by patients.

VM can even keep companies that are dead in the water from sinking any deeper. Consider General Motors. GM has the highest production costs of the Big Three. Roger Smith, CEO, has pledged to slash costs by $10 billion (a reduction of $1,800 per car). Yet, according to CPC Director of Product Purchases, James Sines, upgrading quality must also be a top priority. Current quality problems add 20% to corporate costs.

Sines believes that VM will help GM and its divisions cut costs without compromising quality. Since 1980, GM's Delco Products division has saved $11 million via VM, and has documented another $10 to $12 million in cost avoidances. (Potential savings of $21 million have also been identified.) By introducing VM to vendors, the Saginaw division saved $9 million in purchasing costs (with another $34 million on the drawing board). Saginaw's first VM study saved $5,684,000—an ROI of 47-to-1.

Now, suppose a company isn't just dead in the water—it's DOA. AM International is a 90-year-old firm with sales of about $570 million. After losing $245 million in 1981, it filed under Chapter 11 of the U.S. Bankruptcy Code. D.E.A. Tannenberg, Senior VP and President of the Multigraphics Division, knew what was necessary for corporate survival. "In order to build quality into our products and, at the same time, extract costs, it was obvious that we needed to begin some type of Value [Management] program. Initially, 57 multigraphics employees were trained in Value techniques in a four-day seminar. During this particular seminar, participants identified 96 cost reduction projects with a total of $1.2 million in potential savings. That's $1.2 million in four days . . . ." AM International is now a money-maker.

According to Tannenberg, "Companies not practicing Value [Management] today—especially if they are in financial difficulties—are missing out on a very real opportunity to make long-term improvement in their product lines, provide value to their customers, and make major contributions to improve their profitability in both the short and long term."

Here, Tannenberg gives us the value process payoff in a nutshell. Of course, our one-liners in this chapter don't tell the entire VM story. We can "sell the sizzle" in a single chapter, but it takes longer to digest the steak. That's what we'll do in subsequent chapters. At this point, the important thing to remember is that VM has helped dozens of top companies cut their costs while improving their quality. If Value Management hasn't helped you, it's because you've never used it.

2

VM Defined

THERE ARE ONLY TWO THINGS YOU NEED TO KNOW ABOUT VALUE Management: what it is, and what it isn't.

VM — definition time! — is a formal analytical process that reduces costs and improves quality by identifying the necessary function(s) of a given product/service and finding better ways to provide them.

A typical VM study has seven phases (see Fig. 2-1):

1. Preparing for the study (the preliminaries).

2. Identifying and obtaining relevant data (the Information Phase).

3. Analyzing the function(s) that each project component provides, determining if said functions are necessary, and quantifying their relative importance (the Function Phase).

4. Identifying alternative ways to provide necessary functions (the Creative Phase).

5. Evaluating creative ideas (the Evaluation Phase).

6. Further investigating these alternatives (the Investigation Phase).

7. Recommending cost- and quality-effective changes to management (the Recommendation and Implementation Phase).

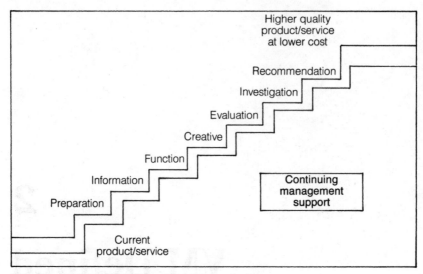

Fig. 2-1. Step-by-step Value Management program

All phases will be described in detail in subsequent chapters.

It is the functional approach—deciding what functions need to be provided and how to best provide them—that separates VM from other management methodologies. Most improvement processes are "tinker techniques." They make marginal improvements in sacred cow products/systems that already exist. VM, however, grabs the bull by the horns and, when necessary, suggests major innovations—like scrapping an unsatisfactory status quo.

Delco used to have a gasket on the radio frequency housing of its antenna shield. The gasket's sole function was to keep water out of the housing. That function seemed necessary until a VM team noted that there were nine other places where water entered the component! One more didn't matter. By eliminating unnecessary functions from the shield, Delco saved more than $1.5 million a year.

Delco didn't improve or refine the gasket. Delco didn't even attempt to make it for less money. Why bother? *The gasket had no useful function.* This function fetish, this ability to separate functional wheat from status quo chaff, is what separates VM practitioners from analytical also-rans.

First-time VM users are often shocked to learn that a product/system component provides negative functions. For instance, participants in the hospital admissions kit study found that one product routinely given to patients was hazardous (it was linked to pneumoconiosis and three kinds of cancer).

Successful product/system components provide only necessary functions and provide them in the most effective manner (cost, quality, efficient, etc.). In his book *Up the Organization*, Robert Townsend conducts a functional analysis of his mythical standard-issue secretary Jane. He notes that the functions she provided (answering phones, scheduling appointments, sorting mail, filing, etc.) were better not provided or provided by other staff members. According to Mr. Townsend, "In my case, unloading a secretary worked out like finding an extra four hours a day."

Thanks to VM, Lincoln Brass Works (Jacksboro, TE) now gets three screws for the price of one. According to Purchasing Manager Harold Ludwig, the company needed three different, but almost identical, screws in its gas burners. The only difference was head style (one was a hex head, one was a recessed Phillips head, and one was a slot head). VM techniques demonstrated that a combination head design would function for all three screwdrivers required on the assembly line at a lower cost (Fig. 2-2). Lincoln now saves $1 per 1,000 screws and has fewer inventory/delivery problems.

Of course, these examples don't tell the entire VM story. Knowing what VM isn't is as important as knowing what it is. Many people read between the methodology's lines, and read things into VM that simply aren't there. A few of the most popular misconceptions follow.

MYTH-TAKE 1: VM is Just Common Sense

To the uninitiated, VM sounds like a megadose of common sense. It is, to a point, but there are pointed differences. Common sense is anything but common. It is a "given" rather than a "learned." VM is a step-by-step process that anyone can follow. "Programmable" common sense, if you will.

Unlike VM, common sense is limiting. It tells us not to mess with success. This circumvents innovations and better alternatives. In *Marketing Myopia*, Theodore Levitt describes a famous Boston millionaire of the early 1900s who believed he had more common sense than his heirs. To guarantee their security, his will stipulated that all his money be invested in electric streetcar securities *forever*. How's that for "security"?

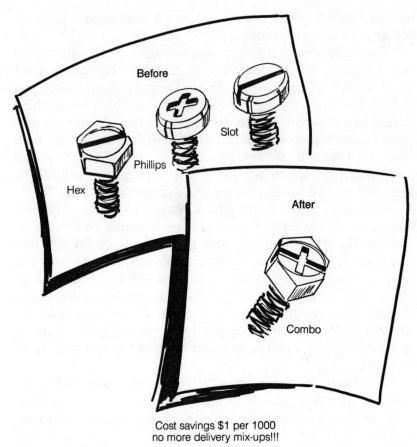

Fig. 2-2. A combination head that functions for all three screwdrivers at a lower cost.

Common sense tells us to take certain things for granted, but it's the people who *defy* current common sense—such as the Wright brothers who thought men could fly—that create new and better realities. When they do, common sense shifts and incorporates the new ideas, which stand until another innovator comes along.

Speaking of flying, Fred Smith, CEO of Federal Express, recently saw through the common sense smoke screen to solve a major problem for frequent flyers: fog. Common sense (well, commonly-accepted sense) had the industry use expensive ground-based systems that help fogbound pilots fly blind. The complex machinery worked about as often as an Arizona snowblower.

One day, an FE employee, Charles Brandon, said, "You know,

what we ought to do is try to see through the fog." In short, give pilots back the "seeing" function. FE's research did a complete 180-degree turn. The company has since developed a system that allows pilots (rather than machines) to see through fog. Smith guaranteed that by 1990 none of FE's planes would ever be fogged in or out again.

Is VM just common sense? Hardly. Would top companies spend millions of dollars a year nurturing a common sense department?

MYTH-TAKE 2:
VM is Just a Standard Review or Cost-Cutting Process

As you'll see, VM requires more sweat equity than a short-and-sweet peer review. If a company president says, "We do VM on everything that goes out of our office," he doesn't know what VM is. Take *your* business out of his office and find somebody who does.

It is also important to recognize that VM *never* cuts costs at the expense of quality. VM's focus is on function. Cutting costs and improving quality are simply ways to provide functions more efficiently. They have equal weight in the VM lexicography.

However, Value practitioners with a mean streak often note that VM does a better job of cutting costs than techniques created for that single purpose. A Value manager at Hughes Aircraft knows of a supplier whose recent cost reduction study on a braided cable saved the vendor 12%. Hughes then used VM to improve cable quality *and* to increase the 12% savings to almost 30%.

MYTH-TAKE 3: Using VM on Current Products/
Services/Processes Implies They were Poorly Designed

Though VM suggests improvements, it never assigns blame or assumes that someone did something wrong. There is no right and wrong, just a good and a better. Often, better alternatives exist because of new technologies or innovations. Initial product designers can't be blamed for failing to use nonexistent technologies!

This myth-take is mostly an attitude problem. A Value practitioner once ran into the Vice President of Engineering at a major electronics firm while visiting at the request of middle management. The VP ordered him off the premises and threatened to fire any employee who got involved with VM. He felt that utilizing VM was the same thing as admitting that his company made a poor product.

As an employer, you wouldn't be impressed with that man's attitude. As a stockholder, you wouldn't be comfortable with a company that believes its product has no potential for improvement. (Over 100 years ago, the U.S. patent office was almost closed because its Director believed "everything has already been invented.")

VM is a tool for the future, not an indictment of the past.

MYTH-TAKE 4: VM Is a Miracle Cure

This assumption just "mythes" reality. VM is an opportunity rather than a miracle cure. It couldn't have saved the buggy whip industry. It can't save a business that is dying for lack of public interest. If management fights VM, VM can't fight back.

If management is going to fight, it should fight *with* VM rather than against it. A company that has bouts with quality problems, has been TKOd by its manufacturing costs, or has generally been taking it on the competitive chin, should have Value Management in its corner. VM can knock out lightweight problems and help make the business a competitive contender.

PRACTICED CORPORATE PRACTITIONERS

This list contains only firms who keep a Certified Value Specialist (CVS) on staff and on call. That is, the committed companies.

Many other firms subcontract VM services or benefit from its secondhand use (see the two Sears studies found in "The Creative Phase" chapter as examples), while others carry out an ongoing VM program sans CVS.

It should also be noted that many governmental groups (the Army Corps of Engineers, the California Department of Transportation, all branches of the Department of Defense, the City of New York, the U.S. Forest Service, etc.) keep value specialists on staff. Additional agencies (Environmental Protection Agency, Department of Transportation, etc.) require a VM analysis on major projects.

AM International
Amoco

Ansul Manufacturing Inc.
B F Goodrich
Ball Aerospace
Bell & Howell
Bendix
Black & Decker
Black and Veatch
Boeing Company
Borg Warner
Brunswick Corporation
CH2M Hill
Caterpillar Tractor Company
Chicago Pneumatic Tool
Cleveland Pneumatic Company
Compugraphic Corporation
Control Data Corporation
Cummings Engine Company Inc.
Data General Corporation
Digital Equipment Corporation
Eaton
FMC Corporation
Ford Motor Company
Freightliner Corporation
Frontier Airlines
Fujitsu Limited
General Dynamics
General Electric
Hewlett-Packard
Honeywell
Hughes Aircraft Company
IBM
Illinois Bell
Ingersoll Rand
Iowa Bearing Company Inc.
John Deere
Johnson Controls Inc.
Joy Manufacturing
LTV Aerospace Corporation
Lockheed
Mack Trucks
Martin Marietta Corporation

McKinsey & Company
Midland Ross Corporation
Morton Thiokol
Multigraphics
NCR Corporation
Nastar
Northern Telecom
Olivetti
Omark Industries
Owens-Corning Fiberglass Corporation
Parker Hannifin
Philadelphia Gear Corporation
Philips Industries
Playskool
Portland Iron Works
Pullman Standard
RCA
Raytheon Company
Rockwell Corporation
St. Regis Paper
Sheller-Globe
Sikorsky Aircraft
Sperry Corporation
Smith & Wesson
Stanley Tools
Stouffers
Sunbeam Corporation
Sunstrand Aviation
TRW
Tektronix
Teledyne Water Pik
Trans World Airlines
Union Carbide
Wagner Spray Technology Corporation
Wang Laboratories
Western Electric Company
Westinghouse

3

The Preliminaries

THIS IS THE COMMITMENT CAVEAT. YES, YOU WANT TO MAKE YOUR business more competitive. Yes, Value Management sounds like the answer to your cares. But don't leap before you look. There's more to VM than meets the overly-enthusiastic eye.

VM is a question of commitment and strength. It will force you to ask tough and occasionally embarrassing questions. To quote one Value Manager, "VM requires willpower and won't cower." The critical query is: when push comes to shove, will you pull away from questions that seem to challenge corporate competence or judgment?

VM is much more than the following questions, but they help illustrate one of VM's biggest problems: the lack of corporate commitment. If somebody in your firm asked these questions, would you say he was open-minded or that he had holes in his head? Would you encourage this kind of head-to-toe soul-searching? In short, are you willing to break away from past mistakes if it means correcting the future?

Many companies are willing to face hard-to-ask questions, and are repaid with hard-to-believe results. Consider the following:

1. Does every function/component of the product/system/ process in question add value?

There are two types of value: use value (something that makes the product work) and esteem/aesthetic value (something that makes the product sell). If a component has neither, it should be eliminated.

As a standard operating procedure, General Electric used to grind the flashing off all bolts. The grinding had a cosmetic/aesthetic function. In the case of a particular bolt, however, the function added no value. This bolt (which was used inside a machine and never seen) had no aesthetic potential, ground or not. Thanks to VM, the "ground rules" were changed, and GE now saves $2,000 annually on that single bolt.

2. Is the value of the function/component in line with its cost?

Are you paying a buck-and-a-half for 50 cents worth of function? At Phillips Industries, one division was building wooden crates out of one-by-three lumber and two-inch staples. A VM study found that employees were using more staples than necessary. New stapling standards saved the company $19,000 a year. By replacing the one-by-three lumber with one-by-four lumber (which met all quality standards), the firm saves an additional $83,000 annually.

3. Does the product/system require all of its components/functions?

It is a simple task to make things complex, but a complex task to make things simple. General Dynamics knows that, and so do its Value Managers. This major defense contractor recently redesigned the fuel pylons on its F-16 jet fighter, thereby reducing the number of parts from 62 to 24. The savings in materials and labor are $20.8 million.

4. Can a standard part, or other substitute, replace a more expensive unit?

The Tri-Wall Company (Woodbury, NY) convinced a sugar beet processor to replace the 100-pound storage bags it purchased from another supplier with a special double version of Tri-Wall's 2,500-pound King Pak. The processor was able to cut labor costs by over 50%, stop product spillage, and cheaply recycle packaging material. Tri-Wall gained a profitable new account.

5. Can you buy a product for less from another supplier?

   When demand for an Eaton Corporation component dropped by 90%, its Controls Division's original volume-run vendor increased the unit price of a special-order air control valve by 1,000%. Eaton found a small-run supplier who cut the cost increase to only 50%.

6. Can the component be made via a less expensive process? Are you making a low-volume product with expensive high-volume methods (or vice versa)?

   Hughes Aircraft cut the cost of standard brass washers from $3.50 each to 6 cents by chemically etching, rather than machining, them (a savings of over 98%).

7. Does a product/system have hidden costs (repair/maintenance, lots of downtime, redundant functions, a poor safety record, product damage, under-utilization of employees, high turnover, high error rate, etc.)?

   Transportation routing at Union Carbide was not only inefficient, it was resulting in substantial in-transit damage. VM helped the firm streamline its transportation line and save $100,000 in the process.

Questions like these are not easy to ask, but VM can only succeed in a firm if the company is willing to ask hard questions and accept some unpleasant answers.

Another important commitment caveat for VM is the ability to motivate employees. VM can improve a company *but only if its employees have the desire to do a better job*. Creating this desire can be tricky. It's like telling a man that he either has to admit that he doesn't want to improve or that he isn't doing the best job possible. Damned if you do, damned if you don't.

Motivation is a function of the business environment. If a Value Manager in the engineering department redesigns a component and reduces its cost by 40%, what would your response be? It might be "Great!" or "Why didn't you design it right the first time?" One response will encourage further VM participation. The other will quickly kill it. A pat on the back beats a kick in the teeth.

A third problem is the preponderance of mental roadblocks in study participants. "Mental masturbation"—the art of making excuses rather than solutions—is a time-honored practice. Art

Mudge of Joy Manufacturing offers a list of subconscious stumbling blocks that he has come across in his value ventures:

- SOMEBODY WON'T LIKE IT. I agree, but—well, operating personnel, middle management, top management, the executive committee, the unions, the customers, or company policy will fight it (e.g., you understand *I'm* not the problem . . .).
- WHO, ME? It's not within my responsibility, job, authority, specialty, interest, etc.
- YOU MEAN, *now*? We don't have the time. We should do some market testing before we make up our minds. We're not up to that just yet. Let's sleep on it, give it some thought. I'll get back to you. Why don't we set up a committee? Let's do a little more study. You're ahead of your time.
- NOT ON *my* BUDGET, YOU DON'T! It would be too expensive. We don't have the people to put it all together. There goes our overhead! It's not in our budget. We don't have budgetary approval. We'll end up losing money. We don't have enough room, equipment, expertise, etc.
- IF ALL ELSE FAILS, BELITTLE. What are you, some kind of radical? What ivory tower did you escape from? Can't you be realistic for a change? It's a good thought; too bad it won't work! This dog has no intention of learning new tricks! We'll get laughed out of the industry. Not this suggestion again! Oh, brother! Where did you find *that* idea! That's about what I would expect from *staff*. Maybe it'll work in some other department/company/industry, etc., but it won't work in mine! We did great without it before, so who needs it? Are you trying to justify your salary or something?
- MISCELLANEOUS MISGIVINGS. It won't work here. That will make our other equipment obsolete. Our company isn't big enough for that kind of thing. We don't know how to do that. It was NIH (not invented here). Cutting costs— that's not my problem! I don't like it. What do other companies do? We're too old to change. That's never been done before, how do you know it'll work? Why bother? So what? I don't understand what you're trying to say. What you're trying to say is . . . .

Pete Megani, of Martin Marietta's Orlando Aeronautics Division, gives people who use these phrases an "Official Roadblock Certificate." This is one way to show a person that he is standing in the way of progress. However, identifying a roadblock doesn't always solve the problem. One roadblock begets another (after all, this is an issue of attitude). The company has to consciously create an atmosphere where change and reassessment are as natural as breathing.

If these preliminary caveats haven't soured you on VM, read on. You've just survived the small print in your dreams to become competitive.

SELECTING THE APPROPRIATE PROJECT

Value projects should only be undertaken when the subject at hand can offer handsome benefits. The few basic rules of thumb that follow can determine whether a given project deserves a thumbs up or a thumbs down.

- The subject should be relatively complicated. "Soft" subjects (systems, procedures and processes) should have at least six steps; "hard" subjects (products, equipment, facilities) should have at least three subassemblies/functional groups, or eight actions/components. At the same time, the subject must be something that people can define and understand relative to its functions/objectives.

    At IBM's East Fishkill facility, VM was used on a fairly complex (numerous components) yet easy-to-understand (single function) mask holder. Six design changes on the holder and its container saved $385,000.

- The subject should be in the planning stages or in current use and able to incorporate recommended changes. It doesn't pay to do VM on a building that is already finished.

    One CVS (Certified Value Specialist) recently studied a major corporate division's metals procurement practices, only to find that his recommendations (which identified potential savings of 40% on crucial alloy elements) were of no value to the company because it had already decided to phase out the division. VM can rejuvenate, but it can't resurrect.

Look for soft or hard projects whose items/operations:

- Are difficult to make, use, understand or do. These are usually easy to identify because they involve too much work/manpower/equipment.

  Inefficient designs are often the poor-value villain. At a major insurance company, typists complained about a complicated workman's compensation form. The typists were to type an "X" in front of any information section that policyholders had to complete. The two-sided, two-page NCR form required typists to remove it from the typewriter at least three times and to align the platen at least nine times.

  The function of the typing was quite simple: to direct policyholders to the proper sections. A VM team redesigned the form so that the single highlighted category at the top of the first page read, "Please fill in sections (blank) on the following two pages." The typists simply filled in the blank with the appropriate numbers. The average time to complete the form dropped from 1 minute, 39 seconds to 7 seconds.

- Are too much of a good thing—too big, too heavy, too complicated, too extravagant. Overkill is overrated.

  A Westinghouse Value Management team in St. Louis studied an industrial load center. "By using Value [Management] techniques in the design function," reported Bob Hufford, Engineering Manager, "we reduced the number of parts in the product by 20% and cut the number of different types of parts by 30%. Assembly time was also reduced by studying the ergonomics of assembly. All this helped us improve product quality and reduce cost."

- Are nonstandard (materials, usage, delivery, sizes, shapes, forms, etc.). Have competitors found a better, or less expensive, way to do what you need done?

  Distilled water is commonly used in blueprint and photographic lab equipment even though local water will often meet purity requirements at a far lower cost. While savings may only run to several hundred dollars annually, implementing the change to tap water is simplicity itself and personnel required for purchasing, delivery, storage, etc. are relieved of unnecessary tasks.

- Are not under your control (e.g., subject to embargo, a vendor's economic health, supply, union problems, a monopolistic seller, etc.)

  Chromium is a crucial industrial alloy found mostly in South Africa and the USSR. Considering political realities, a supplier might attempt to find substitute materials. Alternative energy sources (particularly renewable forms) are also potential VM subjects.

- Have room for improvement relative to a poor profit margin or market share.

  Years ago, GE was losing market share on a cold-storage refrigerator unit because costs were too high. The manufacturing department passed the product on to a VM team with the comment, "We give you this with our tongue in cheek because we don't think that another penny can be taken out of the cost."

  The VM team found that a wire clip used to secure the unit cover was made of phosphor bronze at an annual cost of $7,000. Phosphor bronze is usually specified when a part has to flex millions of times. Since this part was only used six times in the average unit's lifetime, the VM team recommended a change to spring brass. That single revision saved the division $4,000 per year. By specifying laminated plastic for the cover, VM lowered the unit cost from four cents to 1.5 cents, saving an additional $25,000 annually.

- Could be purchased instead of made in-house, or made in-house rather than by another firm.

  Ansul Manufacturing decided to purchase, rather than manufacture, its fire extinguisher shell. The decision cut 10% off shell costs. Thanks to cost-cutting savings, Ansul was able to double its sales the year after the VM study.

It's important to analyze a project before giving it the Value Management treatment. The ultimate irony would be to waste Value Management, a concept designed to prevent waste and inefficiency, on a project that doesn't deserve the time and attention. Time is money. VM time can be a penny saved or a penny spurned.

SELECTING THE VM TEAM

Word has it that when Moses descended from Mount Arrarat, he was actually carrying three stone tablets which bore the 15 commandments. Before he abandoned the third and heaviest stone, Moses skimmed the text, which was subtitled "Business Regulations." And there it was, number eleven, literally carved in stone: "Thou shalt *not* committee."

VM teams are *not* committees or typical business teams. VM teams gather the right people at the right time to ask the right questions about the right things. No miscellaneous managers, no career committee-goers, no time-takers or ego-makers. In Value Management, T-E-A-M stands for "Tough Evaluation of All Members," rather than the all-too-common, "The Experts Are Missing!"

VM teams actually have more in common with professional athletic teams than with standard-issue business committees. For example, in their attempts to draft a winning team, VM leaders use the following four techniques.

Utilize Special Teams

Thinking of a company as a single business is rather misleading. Every firm has divisions that function almost like separate organizations. They run the business of accounting, sales, administration, production, etc. In well-run companies, these components work like a relay team. In poorly-run companies, they aren't even on the same track.

VM recognizes that multidiscipline study teams are necessary to ensure that the needs of all corporate components are met. For example, in the admissions kit study, the VM team had two nurses, a management engineer, a pharmacist, a director of housekeeping, a central supply supervisor, and a material manager. VM teams vary in size according to the complexity of the project and the divisions/areas of knowledge that have a legitimate need for representation.

Luis Venegas of Project Time and Cost (Atlanta, GA) compares VM's multidiscipline approach to professional football teams. VM teams have a qualified leader, usually a Certified Value Manager (quarterback); people representing different divisions/areas of knowledge (halfbacks, tight ends, etc.); VM's formal guidelines (a game plan), and the ability to cut costs while increasing quality (touchdowns). There's only one thing missing—since all of the important departments are represented, there are no after-the-fact, armchair quarterbacks!

Today's businesses are too complex to be run strictly by staff invections or professional line men. To ensure on-line approval and bottom line success, VM teams need both hands-on and knowl-edge-based expertise.

Mix Pros and Rookies

VM team members are usually pros with lots of expertise, but an occasional rookie can liven up the game. A new hire will have valu-able questions about why the status quo works the way it does, questions that old-timers have forgotten. Innocent "whys" can lead to great innovations. The instamatic camera was created because the inventor's granddaughter didn't understand why she had to wait to see the pictures.

Develop Teams, Not Stars

Remember the 1980 U.S. Olympic hockey team? According to sports experts, it won the gold medal by playing "beyond its abili-ties." Like all top squads, it functioned as a team, rather than "every superstar for him or herself."

A team spirit and team attitude are what separate VM squads from VM frauds. Team members must be chosen with care. While it only takes a few negative thinkers to ruin a VM study, it takes more than one or two positive people to salvage a bad-mouthing bevy. To quote Schopenhauer's Law: If you put a spoonful of wine into a barrel full of sewage, you get sewage. If you put a spoonful of sewage into a barrel full of wine, you still get sewage.

Team members need a positive attitude on life, and they either have it or they don't. If a man looks at a partially filled glass and sees it as half full, rather than half empty, he'll make a wholesome addition to the team. If he sees it as half empty, he'd be a poor team player.

Don't waste your time with pessimists. Load your VM team with qualified positive thinkers. The importance of team spirit and positive attitudes cannot be overemphasized.

Share the Strategy

Before each play, a football team huddles to plan its strategies. Everybody knows what the squad is up to. The process makes perfect sense.

Consider this perfect nonsense. Only the quarterback knows the play he is going to run. He whispers it to the center mid-hike, but doesn't share it with the receivers until they are 15 yards down field. The blockers are only told after the fact.

This second scenario doesn't make sense, yet it's the game plan most businesses follow. A winning team, whether it be in sports or VM, needs a winning game plan. An important part of any successful Value strategy is to pack the team with people who can wring out unnecessary costs and run rings around the competition. In short, people willing to grab the brass ring.

SELLING THE VM IDEA

Selecting the best team is important, but it isn't enough. People have to want to play the game.

While VM isn't a hard sell, some selling is required. Value Management means change, and change (even for the better) makes a lot of people nervous. So, proponents should be prepared to answer the question common to all who are not committed, namely, "What's in it for me?"

The question is easy to answer for managers. Most of VM's obvious benefits are in sync with top management objectives: reduced costs, improved quality, greater productivity, improved corporate teamwork and communications, a better work environment, product innovations, creating a conduit for ideas, etc. According to Bill Calhoun, Purchasing Manager for Fletcher Oil and Refining Company (Carson, CA), "As long as management is aware of the positive results of a Value program, it will continue to get support."

Research on corporate Value experience gives some idea of a VM program's sum worth. According to an American Ordnance Association study of 656 Value recommendations, 65% of all recommendations increased product reliability (35% had no effect), 64% enhanced maintainability (36% had no effect), 82% improved producibility (16% had no effect, 2% gave up some producibility to gain a more important benefit), 58% raised human factors (41% had no effect, 1% gave up some human factors to gain a more important benefit), 58% increased parts availability (41% had no effect, 1% gave up some parts availability to gain a more important benefit), 79% shortened production lead time (21% had no effect), 71% benefitted quality (29% had no effect), etc. The list of benefits goes on and on.

Several years ago, the Society of American Value Engineers (SAVE, the professional association that accredits Certified Value Specialists) asked successful companies about their Value programs. The bottom line was this—is a Value program really of value? Since the companies all valued money, efficiency, productivity, personnel growth, etc., the unanimous answer was a definite yes.

According to A.L. Chilstrom, manager of tech-based cost improvement at Allis-Chalmers, the company VM program saved almost $13 million in two years (0.5% of net sales) at a cost to savings ratio of about 1:60. The firm found that its value-verified products "are less costly to produce and more reliable. [They] also have greater quality." Other achieved benefits included "develops personal and leadership qualities in personnel, builds organizational teamwork, improves interdepartment communications, increases productivity, and teaches personnel to be more creative in other work situations."

As one example of program success, Allis-Chalmers' respondents noted that "the company's holdback line was too costly to produce and still be competitive. After VM, a more versatile design halved its weight, tripled its maximum capacity, increased its models from five to 12, all while reducing production costs by 28%."

Cleveland Pneumatic Company also told of ongoing benefits. "Customer good will is enhanced," wrote survey respondents. "We are a major company in our industry (designing and manufacturing aircraft landing gear) and the customers like to know we have an ongoing effort to reduce costs."

Other benefits included: "Team members experience personal growth. Long lasting benefits include improved communications across organizational lines and the feeling that an individual can influence the organization. Also cross-pollenization of knowledge, ideas and feelings occurs."

And then, of course, there is the business bottom line. Value Management helped Cleveland Pneumatic save $750,000 (0.4% of net sales).

Hughes Aircraft has spent $11 million on VM—not bad, considering the $611 million return (3% of net sales). According to W.H. Cooperman, the VM program has enhanced Hughes' market position as follows: "Expands market potential. Enhances competitive position. Allows for the incorporation of new technology. Provides increase in product capability. Reduces contract cost commitments and provides funds for needed change. Keeps the [Hughes] program sold. Deletes unnecessary/costly requirements. Reduces overruns. Improves cash flow. Increases earnings on current and follow-up contracts. Reduces or eliminates non-cost effective requirements." Hughes Aircraft did more than make the *In Search of Excellence* shortlist—it found long-term VM payoffs.

The "What's in it for me?" question is a little more complicated for operating personnel. Often, the question becomes, "What am I in for?" To translate, will increased productivity mean fewer jobs and fewer chances for promotion? Does VM lower costs by cutting salaries? Will VM bring automation or layoffs for unskilled workers?

Let the records show that VM benefits workers in a variety of ways. VM can protect jobs, such as the 10,000 jobs saved at AM International. Stronger, more competitive companies can pay higher wages and offer increased job security. Improved products and methods are a major plus because they increase on-the-job safety and make inefficient tasks less irritating. On-line employees who participate in studies find the chance to substitute a little brain for a lot of brawn refreshing. Some companies pay a percentage of savings for VM ideas. Work environments improve (a Houston hospital that applied VM to its operating room procedures noticed a substantial drop in the turnover of nurses and requests for transfers). While VM can't guarantee that everybody will come out a winner, it bats pretty close to 1.000.

"What's in it for me?" takes on a new twist when it's asked by vendors. Many companies ask their suppliers to participate in VM studies. Freightliner, for example, used to make shift levers for its truck cabs. When it put the component out for competitive bid, TRW was the low bidder, but TRW's bid was $5 higher per unit than Freightliner's own costs. With Freightliner's encouragement, TRW conducted a VM study on the component and made design changes that improved component quality and saved Freightliner $6.50 per unit over its original costs.

Texas Instruments also values vendor ideas. Jack Swincle, TI's Dallas Director of Materials, says that vendors provide about half of the company's total VM savings. At Beech Aircraft Corporation, John Overton estimates 1974 VM savings at over $2 million, 40% generated by suppliers. For 18 years, Hottinger Baldwin Measurements has utilized vendor VM, and has had a 20 to 25% average cost reduction.

Vendors can be a valuable VM asset if they are approached in the right way. Remember—buyers can't insist that sellers use VM. Many vendors will react defensively to the suggestion that they could improve product quality and cut their costs by 30%. Vendor VM requires a little finesse and a lot of support. A good vendor VM program needs at least four components:

1. *Proof positive to the vendor that his help is appreciated.* Some firms (Scott Paper Company, for example) give vendors a "vested interest" in the program by trading vendor assistance for a reduction in competitive bidding and the total number of suppliers. Serious VM studies also include vendors in the process ASAP. It's easier to change a blueprint than a production run.

2. *Good methods to generate ideas.* When talking to current or potential suppliers, new ideas can be solicited. Writing requests for proposals (RFPs) according to function (vs. according to design) is a second winning way. The buyer can pay for vendor VM training. Suppliers can be encouraged to send new product brochures to prime the internal pump. Suggestion forms and letters requesting ideas should be sent periodically to vendor marketing and engineering departments (this is particularly effective when the vendor is given a specific problem to brainstorm). VM displays can be utilized to get suppliers in the mood. Vendor top management is often invited to take a look at what VM has already done for the buyer.

3. *A timely procedure for evaluating vendor ideas.* At Honeywell, initial responses to vendor ideas are always made within 10 days of receipt. The idea is appraised and a first progress report is made within 45 days. Procrastination and VM mix about as well as oil and water. Procrastination may even eliminate a suggestion outright if the need passes before the suggestion can be implemented.

4. *A direct payoff.* Vendors who assist in successful VM studies have a right to expect increased business or some other quantitative reward. Many organizations—including the federal government—use VECPs (Value Engineering Change Proposals) to solicit and repay vendor assistance. Thanks to vendor VM, the Air Force saved $760 million in 1983 while defense contractors were paid a percentage of the savings.

The key to selling Value Management is demonstrating to participants and potential supporters—whether they are managers, employees, or vendors—that VM pays off. The benefits are not a long-shot gamble, they're a documented sure thing. Participants can bet on it.

4

The Information Phase

CONSIDER THE CASE OF THE NO-BARGAIN BRIDGE. A VM STUDY conducted by O'Brien-Kreitzberg (Merchantville, NJ) for Fayette County, PA, discovered that a revised design would "save" $735,300 on a bridge estimated to "cost" only $313,000. Impossible? Not for Value Management.

A proper estimate includes all relevant costs. In this case (which is not an isolated case, to be sure!), the project estimate was incomplete. In addition to the construction bid, it should have included the cost of detouring traffic, strengthening structures along the detour, etc. The original bridge design required a 50-day detour at a cost of $15,000 per day. Rerouting an average daily traffic count of 5,050 vehicles—10% of them heavy trucks—is expensive, irritating, and potentially dangerous.

The VM team discovered that if a box culvert was added to the original bridge design, traffic only needed to be rerouted for six days. Adding the $60,300 saved on bridge construction to the $660,000 saved on detours and $15,000 saved on structural strengthening, the savings totaled $735,300—over twice the original bridge estimate.

Mark Twain once called data "lies, damn lies and statistics." We see statistics as being credible, yet under careful analysis, much of our decision-making data is about as stable as the San Andreas Fault. Here are some relevant concerns.

- *It can be difficult to determine whether a comment is opinion or fact.* Westinghouse's Productivity and Quality Center once conducted a survey of personnel in engineering, purchasing, production, and sales to see if they knew product input costs. No "knews" was good news. Some of the "experts" were off by factors as high as 10-to-1! If a VM study had made decisions based on their cost estimates, it would have been a decisive failure.

- *People go beyond their limits of expertise.* Marketing masters shouldn't pass judgment on production pundits. Experts shouldn't substitute name recognition for reliable research. Unfortunately, temptation is often stronger than justification.

  In 1906, Percival Lowell, a renowned astronomer, made headlines in academic circles by announcing that he had discovered and charted red, moving canals on Mars. His detailed maps, soon a scientific staple, were quickly added to school atlases and other research publications. However, additional outside research found that no such canals exist. Lowell had a rare eye disease ("Lowell's Syndrome") which allows victims to see the veins in their own eyes. Thanks to Lowell's expert status, the mistake was accepted for years.

- *Past opinions affirm but processes improve.* Changes in technology can change realities in business. For example, Aurora Pump (North Aurora, IL) learned through VM that investment casting—a process that was once too expensive to use on its single and multistage pumps—could save the company 60% over its current sand-casting techniques.

- *Pious bias.* Professional perspective can be a boon or a bane when it comes to interpreting facts. In 1984, the Timberland Corporation (a leading producer of high-quality boots) was almost pulled apart by differences between its sales and marketing departments. Using exactly the same data, the sales section "documented" that the company should emphasize low-cost boots while the marketing men "proved" that the firm should opt for the upscale market. Though the marketing moguls won the day (and rebuilt the business), the conflict cost the company a great deal of time and money.

Abundant and reliable data is crucial to valuable VM. Value Managers must have a good grip on the subject at hand. The information phase is critical because, while products/systems exist to give users what they want and need, *those needs may not be well-understood*.

A Value team must question both customer and company-generated requirements/desires. Many will turn out to be based on a lack of options, incomplete or incorrect information, out-of-date technologies, unnecessarily strict tolerances, past problems that are long since solved, inappropriate standards, or out-of-touch traditions. Many products are unnecessarily expensive because people don't know what they need/want.

One major manufacturer's sports watch is guaranteed to tell the correct time "100 meters under water." That's nice, but unnecessary. A person's thorax will collapse somewhere between 30 and 90 meters. People get "dive drunk" at about 40 meters, and a quick surface from that depth can result in the bends or a ruptured eardrum. To quote *New Scientist*, "anyone doing a thorough consumer test on the Citizen Lifestyle watch is likely to end up dead." If a customer pays anything extra for that "extra measure of protection," he's paying too much.

In data collection, the key words to remember are when, what, where, who, why, and how. Value participants try to ask and answer at least 10 such questions about each key category in any relevant specialty. Art Mudge offers the following extensive list of specialties/key categories:

- ENGINEERING: Product history (original need, subsequent needs/options, data of first and subsequent designs, alternative solutions to needs that were considered, design problems/opportunities, changes made in the original and subsequent plans, etc.); patents, trademarks, copyrights and captive materials; requirements for appearance, performance, physical demands, workmanship, maintenance (including raw and finished materials, weight, height, dimensions, tolerances, shock and vibration, environment, life, industrial and insurance rating standards, etc.); use of the product (does it have a single or numerous applications, what volume of the item is used annually, what quantities are ordered, etc.); design modifications or improvements being considered or in progress; items/processes that the engineering department thinks have the greatest cost-effective room for improvement, etc.

- MARKETING: Market requirements, constraints and preferences regarding size, reliability, serviceability (is it a "you're responsible" or a "we'll take care of it"); maintainability, functionality, lifespan, operability, desired or required or retired options, environmental hazards and conditions past, present, and future; documented product history (safety record, market for and reasons for service calls and replacement parts, operating timeliness of products and key parts, complaint and compliment letters, feedback from sales staff, returns due to quality control or other problems, second purchases of the unit, reasons for loss of account, etc.); competitive conditions and sales figures (current and future market size, corporate market share, share of major and minor competitors, anticipated new competitors, regional strengths/weaknesses, elasticity of demand, price sensitivity of market, reasons for and predictions of anticipated gain/loss of market share, etc.); anticipated value of the market (is the market growing, saturated or stagnating, is the product likely to be phased out by new technologies, etc.), items/operations the marketing department thinks would benefit most from VM, etc.

- PURCHASING: General logistic concerns (manufacturing process specs, operation sequence, volume produced, special or standard run, production methods used, necessary equipment/tools/etc. and their life span, age, cost, ownership, availability and comparison to the state of the art technological level); special equipment data (its nature, cost, life span, availability, required support personnel, education/training, etc.); materials utilization (materials needs and related scrap, substitute materials, etc.); statistics on the amount of material that is scrapped, rejected, reworked, misapplied and why (poor quality control, production problems, did not meet stringent tolerances, unacceptable raw material, incorrect shipment, etc.).

If an entire component comes from an outside vendor, consider the source, potential alternative sources (even if never used before), purchasing logistics (order sizes, person who initiates the order, frequency of orders, shipment or destination contracts, yearly contracts vs. output contracts vs. lot quantities, location of manufacturer or warehouse, delivery schedules, add-on costs such as transportation, insurance, unloading, etc.); what areas the purchasing department suggests should be studied for possible VM savings, etc.

This is just the beginning. When the Value team thinks it has all the answers, it needs to ask more questions, such as:[1]

- *Who/what can offer us additional information?* The list is almost endless. Of course, there are corporate insiders and vendor outsiders. Larry Miles (General Electric) recalls an adjusting screw which was so "unusual" that company purchasing agents were sure that no vendor had anything that looked like it. Miles talked to vendors anyway and, sure enough, they didn't. However, two vendors *did* have a unit that could easily replace the 8-cent item for less than one-third of a cent (Fig. 4-1).

   Conversely, corporate insiders once helped Miles cut the cost of an item from $1.27 to 13 cents. By reading trade catalogs, production pros learned that numerous vendors carried an item similar in diameter, thickness, etc., to their in-house spacer hub. The only difference was that the vendor variety (which cost 4 cents) contained no holes and was rounded rather than flat. The on-line experts found that they could flatten the 4-cent hub for 1 cent and could drill the holes for another 8 cents. Unit costs were thus reduced by almost 90%.

   Trade catalogs, directories (subject indices like the *Business Periodicals Index* and *Subjects In Print*, periodicals, house organs, newsletter indices, etc.), professional or trade associations, special library collections, doctoral dissertations, etc., are all valuable sources of applicable information. *Finding Facts Fast: How to Find Out What You Want to Know Immediately* (by Alden Todd, a Morrow Paperback publication) lists 87 different research publications geared to finding data that is valuable but difficult to detect. Research librarians are another valuable resource.

---

[1]These case studies are given only to demonstrate the value of in-depth data. Actual project solutions will not become apparent until later in the VM study.

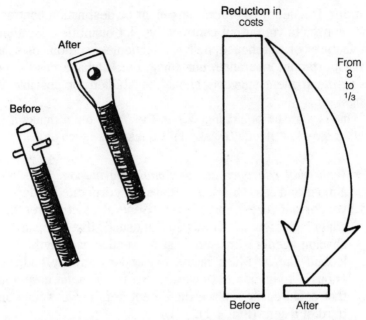

Fig. 4-1. Replacement of this GE screw reduces cost from 8 cents an item to less than 1/3 of a cent.

Just how important are printed research materials? Many industry experts credit Sears' rise to national prominence on its early recognition of changing population demographics. According to legend, the trends were first brought to Sears' attention by a man who was stationed out of the country and had nothing better to do than read old U.S. Census reports.

• *Can anyone deny or verify what we think we've learned via additional data or a new perspective?* In his book *Up the Organization,* Robert Townsend recalls plans he made to create a discount subsidiary (translation: lower-priced competitor) to compete with Avis that would theoretically "increase [the corporate] market share." In actuality, it only would take business away from the profitable parent. Too, in Townsend's words, "verify my own brilliance" he shared his plans with a regional VP who TKO'd the project with a single verbal blow: "I don't know what *you* call it, but we Polacks call that 'pissing in the soup.' " Isn't perspective a wonderful thing?

- *Can anyone offer ancillary information that might be of value?* Computers are great gizmos, but they don't have the ability to pick and choose seemingly random pieces of information and turn them into meaningful questions. Thank heaven for humans!

A branch of the armed forces was building a big-budget, fully computerized inventory storage building. Unfortunately, the budget wasn't as big as the cost estimate. A CVS (Certified Value Specialist) team was hired to review the blueprints (which were based on armed forces "cookie-cutter plans") and cut costs without affecting facility size or construction quality.

One member of the VM team questioned the facility's unusually thick walls. He was told they were needed to prevent serious damage from forklifts, a common problem. "Yes," said the CVS, "but since your facility is completely computerized—including the conveyor belts— *it won't have any forklifts!*" The walls were redrawn to a smaller, but totally adequate, scale. Taxpayers saved millions.

Once the VM team has a full line of production information, it needs to get a line on project costs. Finding out what a current or in-design product/service really costs is much more involved than one might suspect. Art Mudge offers the following partial list.

Potential Costs

(NOTE: These are only applicable for VM projects on unfinished products/services. If a product is finished, these costs have already been incurred; nothing can be gained by analyzing them. Why cry over spilt milk?)

- *One-time labor*: Basic wages, overtime, bonuses, benefits, etc., paid for product design, plant layout, drafting, quality control, production planning/engineering, equipment purchasing, R&D testing and support, field engineering, education and training, initial administrative support, original and subsequent documentation (writing, producing and creating materials such as drawings, specifications, manuals, pamphlets, brochures, contracts, required inventory lists, et al.), etc.

- *One-time materials*: Designing/tooling up special machines/ equipment/tools, prototypes, models and samples; initial test equipment; new packing and handling processes, etc.
- *One-time miscellaneous*: Travel (to study other plants using the process, visit experts, etc.), rental or lease equipment, conversion costs, added costs during tool-up, specialists on contract, scrapping old processes and materials, retrofitting current assets, modifying materials, etc.

Definite Costs

- *Recurring labor*: Basic wages, overtime, bonuses and bene-fits, etc., paid for manufacturing, maintenance, engineering, support services (including administrative, direct manage-rial, clerical, etc.), technical support, field services, docu-mentation/records, quality control, purchasing, shipping and inventory personnel, etc.
- *Product inputs*: Raw materials and assembled goods, sub-contractors, indirect supplies and materials, packing equip-ment/materials, expendable tools, etc.
- *Miscellaneous*: Travel expenses, equipment costs (including computers), outside contractors, shipping costs, inventory costs, etc.

A few things will emerge from the in-depth cost inquisition (other than the desire to take a month's vacation!). Obviously, the greatest potential for cost improvements is in the areas of greatest cost. Would you rather save 30% on a million-dollar doodad or 100% on a 50-cent piece?

Variable costs will present a clear target for cost reduction because of their oversized share of the budget. Large-ticket items will overshadow their low-cost compatriots as potential projects. Secondary costs (costs not directly linked with the important func-tions of the product/system) will also account for large lumps in an overblown budget. In short, the more you know about costs, the better you can target your VM viewfinder.

Remember the no-bargain bridge? Conducting Value Manage-ment with imprecise information is no bargain either. You'll sniff out more benefits than you bargained for if your data is up to snuff.

SUPERIOR SOURCES OF INVALUABLE INFORMATION

If you're going to play ball, you have to know the rules. If you don't, you're going to start the game with three strikes against you.

"Should Have Done More Research" Horror Story #1

When the Celanese Corporation was in the batter's box preparing to enter the paper business in Europe, it not only struck out at the profit plate, it was severely battered. Just look at the scorecard:

- First inning: the company purchased a large eucalyptus tree plantation in Sicily for product pulp.

- Second inning: Celanese constructed a major mill, brick by brick, dollar bill by dollar bill.

- Third inning: the company found and hired hands.[2] Strictly local talent.

- Fourth inning: management came in as designated hitter.

Talk about hit and miss. Upon their first visit to the eucalyptus plantations, the Celanese managers found that their "trees" were only a few inches tall. It would be at least 20 years before the outfield eucalyptus would be big league material. In the interim, raw material recruits from Canada were used to fill the empty inventory benches. The Celanese Corporation lost more than $77 million and posted no winning inning. Where for art thou, research? Or . . .

"Should Have Done More Research" Horror Story #2

Consider the case of the wild zoo bugaboo, where the lack of solid research made a monkey out of a major European conglomerate.

- In their first fall toward financial fallacy, corporate bean counters decided to replace the exotic animals' fancy feed (expensive oranges and bananas) with regular old rutabagas. Just as "real men don't eat quiche," real African animals don't eat rutabagas.[3] The ROI (return on idiocy) was sick

---

[2]It has been suggested that Celanese would have been better served had it held off on the hands and hired some management brains instead. No comment from the author.

[3]Somehow, "Let them eat rutabagas" doesn't have the staying power of Marie Antoinette's famous rejoiner.

and dying animals. Strike one—hunger strike, that is—to management.

- The second sales pitch was to build a luxurious otter pool so that park visitors could be entranced by the mammal's cute animal antics. This otter work, right? Wrong. Ignorant corporate managers bought the wrong kind of otter—a variety that sleeps by day and plays by night (the original party animal). The otters, irritated by all the noisy park visitors who disturbed their sleep, tunneled out and made their escape. Strike, too.

- Third times a harm, er, charm. Showing a great deal of intestinal—not to mention financial—fortitude, the corporate corps decided to spruce up their grey and depressing penguin pool. All it took was a few gallons of fluorescent paint, an inspired artist, and a six figure subsidy. Well, I should say all it took was the poor penguins' eyesight. You see, the Argentinean penguins—who were distinctly designed to live in grey grottos and murky maritimes—went into shock when confronted with "Technicolor tundra." The blindness was temporary, but management's embarrassment was terminal. Strike three, you're out—of the business.

Clearly, the proper research done at the proper time can save money, trouble, and—every bit as important—face. That's why the competent VM practitioner is practiced in the ways of research.

What follows are some of the VM experts' most popular research sources and resources. Most are available at or through your local bookstore, corporate library, public library, state library, or university library. These easy-to-use publications and programs can make your search for the trivial a bit more convivial. But remember, research is a serious business. Take it with a grain of salt—if not with a grain of aspirin.

1. **Alumni Directory** (available from your alumni association).

   Your alma mater matters. Alumni directories allow researchers to keep track of scholastic soulmates who might be willing to make an extra effort for a collegiate colleague.

2. **American Doctoral Dissertations, Dissertation Abstracts International, DATRIX** (an anacronym for Direct Access to Reference Information: a Xerox service), and **Dissertation Abstracts International Retrospective Index**.

   If you want the latest poop on the newest academic scoop, check into this group. They are just what the doctorate ordered.

   • If you know some of a paper's particulars, check *American Doctoral Dissertations*. It checks in with exact dissertation titles, authors, sponsoring universities, and time of publication.

   • *Dissertation Abstracts International* prints 600 word abstracts of concrete works in print. If the paper appears interesting (perhaps you would be willing to settle for "informative"), the full paper can be ordered from University Microfilms (Ann Arbor, MI).

   • DATRIX helps researchers determine if any dissertations have been written on a given subject. There's always the possibility that no serious academician has ever shown an interest in tsetse fly toenails or premium potash.

   • *Dissertation Abstracts International Retrospective Index* lists the dust-gathering dissertations printed between 1938 and 1968.

3. **American Library Directory** (available from the R.R. Bowker Co.).

   This publication lists more than 27,000 libraries geographically and notes anything noteworthy (special collections, archives, activities, memberships, etc.).

4. **American Men and Women of Science** (available from the R.R. Bowker Co.).

   This reference book tells you who knows what (in the sciences of biology, psychology, sociology, economics, political science, etc.) and where to find them. NOTE: Science isn't limited to "natural sciences" (apparently scientists also dabble in the "unnatural"). A corollary work, *Directory of American Scholars*, covers the humanities.

5. **Applied Science and Technology Index** (available from the H.W. Wilson Co.).

   This index follows about 225 subject periodicals and dates back to 1958.

6. **Art Index** (available from the H.W. Wilson Co.).

   This index chronicles about 150 subject periodicals and dates back to 1929.

"Should Have Done More Research" Horror Story #3

In the early 1960s, General Motors tried to market its compact Chevrolet Nova in Mexico. Instead of a get-up-and-go success, the company experienced siesta-slow sales. Why? Nobody had thoroughly researched the name. No va, in Spanish, means "no go." Translation to English: no buyers.

7. **Biological and Agricultural Index** (available from the H.W. Wilson Co.).

   This index covers about 150 subject periodicals and dates back to 1964.

8. **Books in Print** (available from the R.R. Bowker Co.).

   This annual publication lists—by author and title—the 270,000 or so books currently available from publishers. If it's out there somewhere, it's in here someplace. It's some resource!

9. **Center for Research Libraries** (Chicago, IL).

   This center provides a cooperative collection of unusual research materials available only to member institutions. With 3 million plus items, it's closer to one-stop shopping than your local Walmart.

10. **Congressional Directory** (U.S. Printing Office).

    Reciprocity time. You help pay their salaries, they can help you earn yours. This directory lists the members of Congress, Congressional Committees, federal courts and judges, agencies and officers of the Executive branch, etc. These pros have the contacts to put you in contact with the right person/organization. After all, politics is a contact sport.

11. **Directory of Special Libraries and Information Centers** (available from the Gale Research Co., Detroit, MI).

Over 13,000 entries will help the researcher find any and all libraries that specialize in his specialty. Especially helpful.

12. **Editor and Publisher International Yearbook**
    The who's who of editors can help you find the what's what, what's where, or who knows, in whatever field. Why not give them a try?

"Should Have Done More Research" Horror Story #4

In the early 1900s, E.G. Alton and Company—a manufacturer of cigars—saw a golden opportunity go up in a puff of smoke. An erstwhile competitor suggested that the two companies start a joint venture and make a new product—thinly sliced tobacco wrapped in paper—known as "cigarettes."

The proposal was pooh-poohed (or perhaps, puff-puffed) because, in the words of CEO Alton, "Cigarettes will never become popular."

Today, their popularity may be challenged—but not their profitability.

13. **Education Index** (available from the H.W. Wilson Co.).
    This index follows about 240 subject periodicals and dates back to 1929.

14. **Encyclopedia of Associates** (Gale Research Co.).
    This wonderful work lists professional and trade associations by key subject (for example, National Firefighters and Paramedics Association would be listed under "Firefighters" and "Paramedics," not "National"). Most groups encourage quizzical queries.

15. **Gebbie House Magazine Directory** (available from Gebbie Directory, Sioux City, IO).
    If you want to get the inside story, you have to get the inside publication. This directory lists the house organs of many major companies, which can help you organize a search for invaluable inside information.

16. **Government Printing Office Catalog** (available from the Government Printing Office).
    This is your key to unlocking the 27,000 publications printed by the U.S. Government Printing Office. Wonder of wonders, your tax dollars help to make your research work less taxing! Makes you wonder.

17. **Guide to American Directories: A Guide to the Major Business Directories of the United States, Covering All Industrial, Professional and Mercantile Categories** (B. Klein Publications, Inc., Rye, NY).

    That just about says it all.

18. **A Guide to Archives and Manuscripts in the United States** (Yale University Press).

    This aging account is almost ready for the archives itself; but when it comes to pre-1961 perspectives, it's not getting older, it's getting better. For post-1961 information, consult the *National Union Catalog of Manuscript Collections*, the guide's up-to-date data disciple.

"Should Have Done More Research" Horror Story #5

In the late 1970s workers were performing regular maintenance work on the Chesterfield canal near Retford, England. Just before lunch, their dredging drudgery dug up the end of a ponderous iron chain which, in the opinion of the foreman, needed to be removed for safety's sake.

The crew heaved, hoed, winched up the chain, and went to lunch. When they returned less than an hour and a half later, they found the whole canal high and dry. They had, as the saying goes, "pulled the plug." Literally. Take two ulcers and call me in the morning.

19. **Guide to Reference Books**—aka **Winchell's** (available from the American Library Association, Chicago).

    This research librarian's "Bible" is available to us heathens at most local libraries.

20. **Index to Legal Periodicals** (available from the H.W. Wilson Co.).

    This index follows about 325 legal periodicals/bar association journals all the way back to 1908.

21. **Information Industry Association (Washington, D.C.).**

    This association is an excellent interface between high-tech, for-profit information organizations and no-tech, for-knowledge researchers. If ever the twain shall meet, it will be at this twain crossing.

22. **Interlibrary Loan Program**

    This program (run primarily through local public libraries) allows a researcher in one part of the country to borrow hard to find books from libraries in parts unknown. It's kind of a partners-in-print program.

23. **Library of Congress** (aka **LOC**).

    Remember the political paradigm, ''A billion dollars here, a billion dollars there, a pretty soon we're talking about real money''? Well, when it comes to the LOC and its 15 million plus books and pamphlets, we're talking about a real library. And you don't have to be in Washington to use it. You can:

    • get help from your Congressman

    • utilize a research agent headquartered in Washington D.C.

    • write to the General Reference and Bibliography Division of the LOC or

    • use the LOC catalog cards which are found in many public libraries. These are printed in reduced size— three to a page—and bound together into a rather imposing publication.

24. **Library of Congress Cards**

    Researchers can buy complete LOC subject sections from the Card Division, Library of Congress, Building 159, Navy Yard Annex, Washington, D.C., 20541. Query about costs before committing yourself. Knowledge doesn't come cheap (but it does cost less than major mistakes!).

"Should Have Done More Research" Horror Story #6

In the early 1960s, Simmons and Company, which manufactures high-quality beds and mattresses, decided that exporting overseas was the wave of the future. They singled out a ship of state and shipped their ware-with-alls to Japan.

Four years later, the company was at a loss to explain its heavy losses in the island market. The answer—given a little research— was a given. Simmons' product never had a chance. The Japanese don't use beds. They sleep on matlike futons. No wonder Simmons product push was a real sleeper.

25. **National Directory of Newsletters and Reporting Services** (available from Gale Research Co.).

    Consider this a valuable guide to little literatures with big benefits. You can't tell a book by its cover and you can't tell a journal's value by its circulation. Good things come in small packages.

26. **Newspaper Indices.** *The New York Times Index, Wall Street Journal Index, The Times (London) Index, Christian Science Monitor Index,* etc.

    These indices—which help researchers locate specific articles from the named publication—are so easy to use, even the rawest researcher can easily be paper trained.

27. **Out-of-Print Publications**

    These can often be found through:

    - book search specialists
    - out-of-print specialty bookstores
    - the *Guide to Reprints* (NCR/Microcard Editions, Washington, D.C.), and/or
    - reprinters (see *Scholarly Reprint Publishing in the United States,* R.R. Bowker), and/or
    - University Microfilms (Ann Arbor, MI) which copies out-of-print publications out of its files for a modest (considering the value, some would say "dirt cheap") fee.

    NOTE: Out of print is not always analogous to out of date or outrageously expensive.

28. **Paperbound Books in Print** (available from R.R. Bowker).

    This index lists more than 90,000 paperbound books by subject, title, and author. If you're hardpressed to buy a hardbound book, you're bound to find what you want on paper. In paperback.

29. **Polk's City Directories** (available from R.L. Polk Co., Detroit, MI).

If you want information on a particular city's particular resident (age, address, marital bliss or lack thereof, job, employer, phone number, etc.) or business (profession or industry, corporate officers, etc.), this is where you get the party's particulars. It is the city nitty gritty.

30. **PR Bluebook** (PR Publishing, Meridian, NH) or **O'Dwyer's Director of Public Relations Firms** (O'Dwyer Co., Inc., New York, NY).

Contrary to popular belief, PR doesn't stand for "Polished Rhetoric" or "Part Real." These directories list hundreds of "PRos" and their major corporate clients. PR firms can often get you the information you want in PR—in a "Priority Rush."

NOTE: If the client in question has changed hands, you can find out who's currently holding their hand by contacting the Information Center of the Public Relations Society of America, 845 Third Ave., New York, NY 10022. It keeps a handle on such things.

"Should Have Done More Research" Horror Story #7

In 1984, John Worrell Keely had a million dollar idea: a new fuel called vibratory energy. According to Mr. Keely, vibratory energy could power engines to run at 800 rpm for over two weeks, using only a token thimbleful of water for fuel. He even had working models to show Wall Street speculators.

The investors poured in. Pour people. They didn't do enough research. Keely got his million dollars and his investors got the shaft. After Keely's untimely death in 1898, the investors found that they had been two-timed. His "vibratory energy" models were fueled by compressed air and a system of hidden brass tubes, not by the supposed new technology. The fuels and their money were soon parted.

31. **Reader's Guide to Periodical Literature** (available from Reader's Guide).

This is the general use everyman's guide to everything in general. This reference work makes it easy to locate current and past articles from over 150 popular magazines and journals.

32. **Reference Books:** *A Brief Guide* (available from Enoch Pratt Free Library, Baltimore, MD).

    This book is to researchers what all-you-can-eat buffets are to weight watchers. More goodies than you can use! Indispensable.

33. **Social Sciences and Humanities Index** (available from H.W. Wilson Co.).

    This index follows about 205 periodicals dating back to 1965.

34. **Special Libraries Association (SLA) Directories**

    Many local SLA chapters have summarized their local lineups chapter and verse.

35. **Subject Collections:** *A Guide to Special Book Collections in Libraries* (available from R.R. Bowker Co.).

    This publication lists libraries dedicated to a single subject, special collections housed at general libraries, etc. Entries are listed by subject and further broken down by geographical area. If you know what you want and where you are, you'll know where to go.

36. **Statistical Abstract of the United States** (available from the U.S. Printing Office).

    You can ensure that your VM recommendation isn't immediately tabled by backing up your theories with information from these exhaustive statistical tables. It's got information about demography, economics, business, finance, population, social statistics, etc. Come with caffeine. It can be a real smorgas bored.

"Should Have Done More Research" Horror Story #8

A well known speculator owned a half interest in the fledgling facility that made Coca-Cola. He decided he was unimpressed (it should be noted that the investor had never actually *tried* the drink). How could any product succeed with such a maladroit moniker?

Sans research, the investor sold his shares and bought something with a brighter (e.g., better sounding) future: the Raspberry Cola Company. No doubt, his heirs would like to give the old guy a few raspberries. With a Bronx cheer thrown in for good measure.

37. **Subject Headings Used in the Dictionary Catalog of the Library of Congress**

   This reference work indexes all of the call subjects and call numbers used by the Library of Congress. A noble calling. (NOTE: if you want to exhaust all of the research possibilities (and probabilities), check the Library of Congress Classification Schedules, which lists all of the subtopics related to a general topic).

38. **Subject Guide to Books in Print** (available from R.R. Bowker).

   This publication lists—by subject—the 270,000 or so books available in any given year. The 42,500 subject headings should offer something (or many somethings) for everyone.

39. **Thomas Register of American Manufacturers** (Thomas Publishing Co., New York).

   Anybody who is anybody is listed here with everybody. The register is catalogued by product, but additional information is available on geographic location, business size, product trade names, corporate divisions and subsidiaries, etc. You'll even find unabashed advertising.

40. **Ulrich's International Periodicals Directory** (available from R.R. Bowker).

   Ulrich's prints the title, address, age, circulation, frequency, editor, etc., of over 40,000 international magazines and journals. For "enquiring" and acquiring minds.

41. **United States Government Organization Manual** (U.S. Printing Office).

   This publication gives you the lowdown and dirt on all the agencies in the federal government's executive branch. The who, what, when, where, why, and how of government goings on.

42. **World Almanac**

   This is one of the absolute best sources for general in-the-ballpark information. If you aren't sure that you're heading in the right direction, this publication can help you get the proper heading.

5

The Function Phase

THE FUNCTIONAL APPROACH IS WHAT SEPARATES VM FROM ALL other management methodologies. Most corporate improvement committees—whether their goal is to cut costs, improve quality, increase productivity, etc.—are essentially babes in the woods who are trying to run before they learn to walk.

Most improvement techniques examine a fully developed product or system and try to figure out a way to make it cheaper, better, etc. The committees don't go back to square one and define product needs or challenge today's designs. They blatantly assume that the product performs all required functions efficiently and effectively and that any problems are purely peripheral (we could find a cheaper supplier, substitute a cheaper material, etc.). Instead of creeping and crawling through informational insight, fiddling with functions, and cruising through the Creative Phase, they try to hit the floor running. And that's exactly what they do—hit the floor. *Splat*.

Functional analysis, however, takes the improvement process one step at a time. First, the Information Phase gives the VM team the background it needs to ask intelligent questions and get meaningful answers. Second, the Function Phase identifies the vital components of a product/system (what it must and/or should be able to do). Third, the Creative Phase gives us insight into how we can provide these functions in the most effective and least expensive way. This one-foot-at-a-time technique is the reason that VM is a good competitive step in the right direction.

The first task in the Function Phase is to define *all* product/system functions—*important or immaterial*—using two words: a verb (what does it do) and a noun (what does it do it to). The examples are endless: provide weight, filter force, absorb heat, increase prestige, and so on.

STEP 1: *All* Functions Should Be Listed on the Function Format Worksheet

A single component can contain dozens of functions. Even a simple pencil has at least five (make lines, hold medium, protect medium, hold eraser, provide advertising). It can be difficult—and it is definitely time-consuming—to detect all component functions. Still, the VM team needs to identify everything that an item does on the Function Format Worksheet (Fig. 5-1).

Quantity		Function		Function		Additional Comments
Used	Name	Verb	Noun	Basic	Sec.	

Fig. 5-1. Function Format Worksheet.

Time-consuming though they are, these definitions offer big benefits. Simplifying a function to only two words improves communication, analysis, and comprehension. An objective noun and an objective verb leave little room for subjective argument or misunderstanding. If a product/system can't be *completely* described via a variety of two-word combinations, it needs to be divided into smaller components. It's easier to study a heating element, an on/off switch, an interior light, etc., than it is to analyze an entire oven en masse. Direct definitions force the team to get down to brass tacks and really tackle the crucial components—the necessary functions—of a product/system.

No bones about it, VM's focus on what needs to be done as opposed to how things have been done in the past is the backbone of VM benefits. As an example, the Interstate 90 floating bridge in Seattle presented a major design and cost problem because standard 106-foot-wide pontoons (function: float structure) wouldn't fit through Lake Washington's 80-foot-wide navigation locks. Consulting Value Specialists (Portland, OR) focused on current component needs (e.g., functions) rather than on past-date designs. CVS's designed a folding pontoon which provided the same "float structure" function and helped cut the bridge's estimated cost from $70 million to $51 million.

STEP 2: All Functions on the Function Format Worksheet Are Categorized as Work or Sell Functions

There are two distinct functional forms: work functions and sell/esteem functions. Work functions describe an action (conduct electricity, retard growth, slow absorption, etc.). Sell functions cause a product to be more saleable (increase prestige, improve appearance, etc.). Both functions are important. If an item doesn't work, it won't sell. If an item won't sell, who cares whether it works or not?

The functional forms require different kinds of words. Obviously, if something is happening (action) it can be measured. Work functions *always* contain measurable nouns and active verbs. Verbs (absorb, activate, amplify, apply, change, collect, conduct, connect, contain, control, cover, create, emit, enclose, establish, filter, hold, impede, induce, insulate, interrupt, modulate, prevent, produce, protect, provide, rectify, reduce, reflect, repel, separate, shield, strengthen, support, transmit, transfer, etc.) fill the work bill. Quantitative nouns (circuit, current, damage, density, energy, flow, force, fluid, friction, heat, insulation, light, liquid, oxidation, protection, radiation, repair, storage, voltage, volume, weight, etc.) are used to measure how effectively the work function is provided.

Sell or esteem functions are the opposite of work functions.

They employ nebulous nouns and inactive verbs. An unmeasurable something exists (vs. this specific item does this specific thing). The unquantifiable character of a sell function doesn't detract from its importance. Nouns (appearance, beauty, comfort, convenience, effect, exchange, fashion, features, form, identify, importance, prestige, status, style, symmetry, etc.) and verbs (appear, decrease, feel, exist, improve, increase, look, seems, show, etc.) needn't be measurable to have an impact. A diamond doesn't add any work function to an engagement ring, but it sure works wonders for saleability!

The differences between work and sell functions are more than semantic—they're gigantic. For example, if a particular function doesn't help the product work, it is by default a sell function. However, if the noun and verb that describe the function are measurable/active, then the function is unnecessary (e.g., it neither sells the product *or* helps it work). It only adds a needless cost.

Another benefit of this semantic separation is that, once we define functions, we can determine their individual costs. What does it cost to "conduct electricity" or to "insulate wire"? Are we paying more for functions than they are worth? Are we getting a buck's work of esteem for a buck-and-a-half? Is there a less expensive means to the same functional end?

At PowCon's major manufacturing facility in Tempe, AZ, a VM team studied the company's new welding power supply unit with an eye toward improved quality and lowered costs. The unit contained over 75 electrical terminals which cost a minimum of 65 cents apiece. Their function? Electrical connection. The VM team found that the electrical connections, costs, quality, and design would be improved if some terminals (specifically those used on heavy, solid copper wires) were eliminated! Flattening and piercing the ends of the heftier wires allowed them to function as their own terminals. The team also learned that insulation was unnecessary on 90% of the unit's insulated terminals. As a result of these changes, PowCon cut terminal costs by more than half (Fig. 5-2).

STEP 3: All Functions on the Function Format Worksheet Are Labeled as Primary or Secondary

Primary functions are a product's reason for existing, and secondary functions are usually peripheral pluses (primary function by-products or design decisions). Components have only one primary purpose.

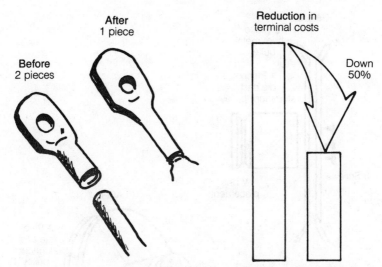

Fig. 5-2. PowCon cut terminal costs more than half with this change.

This functional fission offers favorable fallout. Identifying primary and secondary functions helps highlight what is important (what do we have because we need it and what do we have "just because"?). A large Ohio manufacturer made its pulleys out of scrap metal. It was a good idea gone bad. True, the pulleys cut down on the scrap pile, but they often came loose, causing major problems. A VM team recognized that the pulley's main function should be to change direction or to transmit power, not to use up scrap metal. The team designed a new single-cast pulley that was more reliable and cost 90 cents per unit less than the scrap crap (Fig. 5-3).

Once the functions are defined—identified as work- or sell-related, and categorized as primary or secondary—a few truths will start to emerge. Our designs may be internally inconsistent (e.g., we inexplicably use numerous kinds of metals or processes for a single component). Our products/systems may provide unnecessary functions or provide marginal functions at an exorbitant cost. Some products may be overdesigned (providing more of a function than necessary) or underdone (a single function may be inefficiently divided among numerous components). In short, status quo designs may have little or nothing to do with efficiently meeting status quo needs.

At an Alamo, TN plant, a VM team redesigned an oil instrument transformer. They literally turned it upside down! The im-

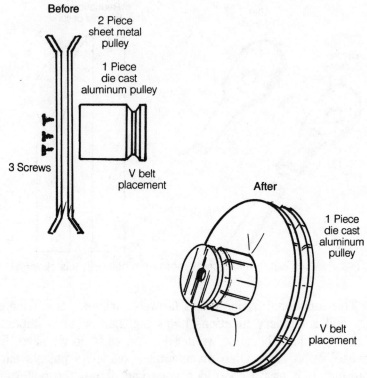

Fig. 5-3. Manfield Products pulley.

proved design used 75% less conductor material and 50% less electrical steel. Though these dramatic savings in material costs were offset by increased labor costs, the design still saved an impressive 42% on the total product cost.

STEP 4: Compare and Quantify the Interrelationships and Importance of the Individual Functions

These are best uncovered by using a Function Appraisal Worksheet (Fig. 5-4). Every function is given a letter. In box AB, function A is compared to function B. If A is more important than B, an A is written in the box and the difference in importance is weighted. If A is much more important than B, the box should contain the notation A-3. If the difference is of medium importance, the weigh-in is 2. If the two functions are of similar importance, the weight drops to a 1 (it might help to know that the longer it takes to weigh two functions against each other, the more likely it is that they are very close in importance).

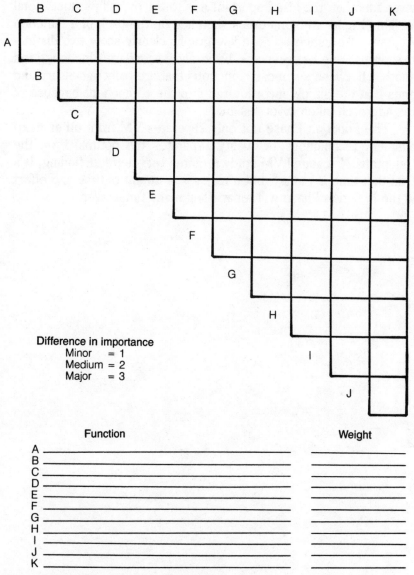

Fig. 5-4. Function Appraisal Worksheet.

Once every function has been compared to every other function, all are given a total weight. If A appears in four boxes with the numbers 1, 3, 2 and 2, its total weight is 8. The number 8 should be written on the weight line corresponding to function A.

The function with the highest total weight is the basic function of the component being analyzed. The lower the total weight of any given function, the less important it is to the overall product. Total Weight Graphs are sometimes sketched on the back of a Function Appraisal Worksheet. These line graphs clearly show two distinctive drops: one between the basic and secondary functions, and another between secondary functions that are truly necessary and ones that are simply incorporated into the component because of the approach taken in its design.

The Function Phase not only separates VM from other management techniques; its quality separates the optimal from the "sloptimal." A sound VM study requires very deft functioning. It's true that time is money, but a major investment of time and effort in the Function Phase will repay itself many times over.

6

The Creative Phase

THE "CREATIVE PHASE" OF VALUE MANAGEMENT IS A MISNOMER.
Many people equate creativity with sudden comprehension, a mental grenade with incredible impact. To them, its origin is unclear, its appearance unpredictable. They're awe-struck at a stroke of genius.

Actually, creativity vis-à-vis VM is easily explained.[1] All creative thought is a function of imagination, inspiration, or illumination. Thanks to VM's functional format, all three techniques are easily tapped.

Take imagination, for example. Imagination is the ability to consciously take what we know and to apply it in new ways to new things. However, knowing where to apply what information is a big brainstorming bugaboo.

A typical cost reduction or quality improvement program will include the question, "How can we cut costs/improve this machine?" (NOTE: This hands-off approach doesn't help determine which data is necessary or what to do with it.)

On the other hand, VM doesn't leave the application of information to chance. VM asks something like, "We need this component to meet the function 'fasten materials.' How many ways can we fasten something?" Suggestions might include welding, nuts/

---

[1]For information about the creative process, a list of reference works is included in The Brainstormer's Bibliography at the back of this book.

bolts, glue, screws, interlocking materials, laminants, snaps, a material binding, tongue-and-groove joints, magnets, nails, buttons, etc. (One participant in a TRW study actually suggested "chewing gum" to meet this particular function!) In short, by tightly channeling the imagination of participants, the flow of ideas is more relevant.[2]

The brainstorming process ("How many ways can we . . .?") spurs inspiration, the second creative process. Inspiration is an aberrant accident. Somebody says something, we see something, or become aware of something that gives us a new idea. Inspiration is really something special, but is not unusual in the VM vista. Again, VM's targeted techniques help practitioners put the proper privity into play. Often, one person's imaginative idea will prompt another's inspiration.

Illumination is a function of deliberate thinking followed by the unconscious "aha syndrome." This description fits VM to a T, because the functional focus involves deliberate thinking and the brainstorming process prompts spontaneous participation.

In short, creativity via-a-vis VM is basically a result of dissecting and understanding a function (problem/need) and then applying knowledge, experience, etc. to it. No hocus-pocus, just a better focus.[3]

Too many problems in business are poorly defined and overly complex. "We need to improve this. We have to make this cheaper. We must increase productivity." These common commandments are closer to prayers than they are to strategies. They are "do nows" without any "how-to's." Since they offer no direction, no explicit benchmarks/goals, no means—not even any *hints*!—they usually don't generate much more than a few "fighting words" memos (or a meaningless motto like, "Work smarter, not harder").

---

[2]At this point in the VM study, members are looking for creative ideas, not necessarily workable ones. The Evaluation (judgmental) Phase is separate from the Creative Phase. We don't want to plug the creative flow by passing premature appraisals.

[3]For some VM participants, a little gamesmanship may be in order. Art Mudge suggests a number of creativity calisthenics. The Rule of 24: Try to be creative in all facets of your life for a full day. The Rule of 25: Work until you come up with 25 ideas about every problem (they don't have to be good, just numerous!). The Rule of 26: Take each letter of the alphabet and try to come up with a problem solution that starts with each letter (actually, The Rule of 20—which excludes Q, U, V, X, Y and Z—would probably work just as well!).

Common corporate practice and VM are as different as hot and cold. The mundane *modus operandi* is to give the business committee a project panacea ("See if you can cut costs on this $100,000 machine") and pray that it can do as you ask. This is the L.U.C.K. (Ludicrous Use of Committee Knowledge) approach. There can be no guarantee of success.

VM substitutes cold logic and directed creativity for lukewarm luck. By defining problems/needs as specific functions, VM directs—and sometimes even leads—practitioners to practical solutions. Team members are able to find low-cost/high-quality alternative means to functional ends.

A VM team might divide that $100,000 machine into 45 components with 500 functions, and then analyze/brainstorm/argue/critique/etc. each function carefully. Team members consult house and vendor experts, research institutes and professional organizations, trade catalogs/reference works, etc., to learn if necessary functions can be provided more cheaply and/or better via different technologies, layouts, materials, designs, vendors, standards, processes, etc. (NOTE: Since VM questions are targeted and specific—"Does X provide function Y?"—it is easy to get specialist input.)

The primary function of one wire in that $100,000 machine might be to "conduct electricity." How could this function be improved? While there are numerous areas for improvement (changes in dimension, precedent order, quantity, motion, the time element, cause/effect, form, character, state or condition, etc.), an examination of only one—a change in materials—will give a general idea of the complexity involved.[4]

- Are conductive materials available that are safer, more reliable, or longer lasting?
- Are any less expensive and/or more cost-effective (why use wire designed to last 100 years when the overall component will only last 10)?
- More resistant to heat/cold?

---

[4]Though the following questions deal specifically with wiring, there are other ways to conduct electricity. These ways and means lead to additional questions. What other conduction methods exist? Would they meet all necessary functions? Again, remember that the critical evaluation of method advantages/disadvantages, costs, quality, etc., are irrelevant in this phase of VM.

- Easier to work with?
- Available from numerous suppliers on a more convenient/ reliable basis?
- Able to speed the transportation of power?
- Is insulation required? If so, are we using the right kind of insulation?
- Will color-coded wires ease production?
- Are we using expensive color-coded wire where it serves no purpose? Might a change in wiring materials allow a wire to meet more than one function (e.g., if we specify thicker wire, then flatten/pierce both ends, can these ends also function as terminals)?

And so on.

There are dozens of questions to ask about virtually every function. However, thanks to VM's "nibbling" functional approach, team members don't bite off more than they can chew. This is critical. Inside every large problem are many small problems (the basic functions) struggling to get out. By focusing on functional molehills, VM allows the mountains (overall quality, cost, productivity) to take care of themselves.

VM teams brainstorm by asking general questions. Such questions are relatively easy to answer (which starts the Creative Phase on the right foot), help kickstart the imagination, and—most importantly—allow team members to identify the specific subject areas which require intense investigation.

Four areas into which these questions may fall appear below along with examples.

THE ME METHODS

Would I have provided this function in this way (or the corollary, would I spend my own money this way)? Is there anything about this product/system that I dislike or that annoys me? Is there something I would like to add to or subtract from the product/system? If I were using this product/system, what would cause me problems? Given a choice, would I use this product/system or substitute (blank)? What does this product/system do to me, for me, against me?

THE COMPETITIVE CRITERIA

What do our competitors use? Do their products/systems provide more, better, less expensive, more reliable, safer, etc., functions? Do they make product/components in-house? What do they do differently and why? What are the advantages/disadvantages? Why do customers stay with us or desert our design? What have customers told us about our competitors' products/systems that they think is important? Do competitors use an item/component/function that costs less? Why the difference?

THE FUNCTIONAL FREE-FOR-ALL

Is the function itself really important (e.g., it inherently valuable or is it dependent on some other variable)? Could we add extra functions or take away unnecessary ones? Would it matter very much if a function were eliminated? Can we quantify a function's importance (or is it a gangling given)? Can we provide the function in a better way (safer, easier to use/produce, more saleable, more workable, less expensive, longer life span, more efficient, using better (more accessible, longer wearing, more functional, etc.) materials, easier to maintain, more reliable, etc.)? Can we add more value to the product/system/function (more work or sales value)? Can we channel numerous functions into one component? Can we divide a function among components? What would happen if there was more or less of this function? Can we learn anything by defining what the function/product/system isn't?

THE MISCELLANEOUS MEANS

Should we buy the product (same/new vendor?), make the product, or buy an unfinished product? Can we make the product more energy efficient (reduce power loss, energy usage, utilize a cheaper power source, etc.)? Can we recycle packaging, by-products, old machines, etc.? Are we using the best possible layout? Is our subject state-of-the-art, or is it state-of-the-past (thanks to corporate custom, trade traditions, uninformed opinions, immaterial materials, etc.)? If we were starting from scratch, could we/would we meet the necessary functions in other ways?

Numerous companies have benefitted by asking function-focused questions. The following are a random sampling.

So, can we improve the quality/cost/value of the subject by changing product/component dimensions? Can we:

1. CHANGE THE LENGTH. Chrysler's K cars were specifically limited in length to no more than 176 inches. Why? So that the cash-starved company could cut transportation costs (more units fit on a standard railroad freight car). This "give or take an inch" approach allowed the company to take higher profits without giving up quality. Thanks to "valued" vehicles, Chrysler was able to repay $813,487,500 on its government guaranteed loans seven years before they came due.

2. CHANGE THE SIZE. Project owners saved $19,800 on the Westridge Mall Sears store (Phoenix, AZ) by replacing four-inch masonry blocks with eight-inch blocks (eight-inch blocks required less masonry, less labor, and cost less per square foot). Like many VM changes, this one was easily implemented ("four" was replaced in the building specifications with "eight"). This was just one of many VM project recommendations. Total VM savings for the project were more than $157,000.

3. CHANGE THE THICKNESS. Sometimes, in the thick of things, VMers discover thinly disguised waste. Union Carbide found that fabricating metal covers from unnecessarily thick stock was cutting into thin profit margins. By changing from 0.043-inch material to 0.036, the firm saves $20,000 a year. Union Carbide, which implemented a company-wide VM training program in 1983, clearly expects Value savings/improvements to strengthen profits.

4. CHANGE THE ORIENTATION (VERTICAL/HORIZONTAL) or 5. CHANGE THE ORIENTATION (INVERT/REVERSE/ETC.). VM can be a topsy-turvy technique. Westinghouse's Components and Instrument Transformer Plant cut the cost of a specialized transformer by over 40% by redesigning the component upside-down. According to Engineering Manager Irv Hansen, the new design is more competitive and accessible to new markets. By capitalizing on inventory flexibility and common parts, production lead time was cut in half.

Clearly, a change to *"that* end up" ended with greater profits (Fig. 6-1).

6. CHANGE THE POSITIONING (SLANTED/PARALLEL /CROSSWISE/ETC.) Everybody has an angle, and VM

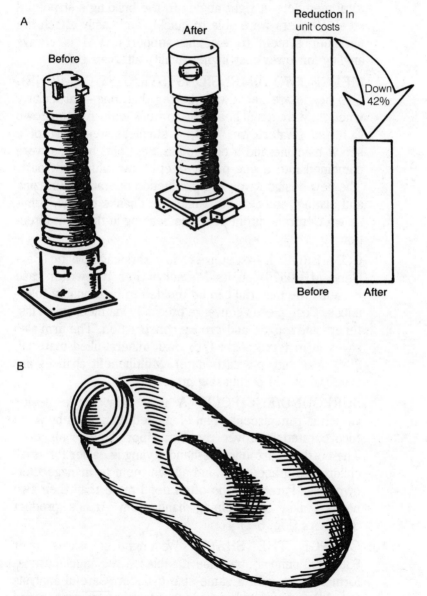

Fig. 6-1. Westinghouse oil transformer and better baby bottle.

makes some angles more profitable than others. Sprinkler system installation costs on a Sears store in Flagstaff, AZ were cut by 20% when VMers redesigned it to run perpendicular to the original design. The system itself was not changed, but this rotational reorientation put structural members at right angles to the building's structural steel. Workers were able to quickly and easily attach the sprinkler system to existing supports. VM is always angling for lower cost/higher quality alternatives!

7. MERGE TWO DIMENSIONS (STRATIFY/COMBINE). Two heads are not always better than one—particularly when they are a real headache to work with. At Johnstown Controls (Watertown, WI), a stainless-steel part of a screw machine and a cold-rolled steel punch press were combined into a one-piece, deep-drawn aluminum part. The new design saves two production operations (brazing and plating) and $35,000 annually. Thanks to VM, Johnstown Controls' profit profile is heading in the right direction.

8. CONVERGE. Xerox utilizes a low-shrinkage plastic (Bayblend MH-6570) on its Memorywriter typewriter case because the material can be molded to high quality tolerances. Case pieces converge precisely via mechanical fasteners and tongue-and-groove construction. The firm also saves in material costs (7% over mineral-filled material, 20% over pure polycarbonate). Multibenefit changes are type-ical of VM purchasing projects.

9. SURROUND/ENCIRCLE. A new baby bottle design (which is reminiscent of an elongated doughnut) by Ansa Incorporated improves the "transport liquid" function. The bottle's surround-the-hand styling is easier for small children to grasp/carry and allows them to manage their own milk. Parents—who often need more than their two hands—value this helping hand from Ansa's product designers (Fig. 6-1).

10. CHANGE THE SHAPE. Westinghouse saves over $350,000 annually because it replaced rectangular transformer tanks with a same-size cylinder. Careful analysis found that the cylindrical shape was more efficient, saved oil, could utilize the same gauge for all tank sizes (differ-

ent rectangular sizes required different special order gauges), could use a smaller/less expensive drain valve, and weighed less (e.g., could be made from thinner steel and required less bracing). All cylindrical tank models could utilize a standard 56-inch diameter whereas different-size rectangles necessitated variable lengths, widths, and heights. The VM team also found that some wide rectangular tanks required special trucking permits (an additional expense).

Can we improve the quality/cost/value of the subject by changing the character of the product/component? Can we:

11. MAKE THE PRODUCT STRONGER/WEAKER. Consumer-oriented companies said, "Let there be light," and new products lit up the cash registers: light beer, light diet foods, light wine coolers, light on the caffeine/sugar/acid/sodium/cholesterol/fat/spices, and so on. Is there a consumer left who hasn't seen the "light," or any consumer-serving manufacturer who hasn't seen the potential profits?

12. ALTER THE CHARACTER. At Amoco's oil refinery in Texas City, TX, obsolete and surplus equipment was sold to local scrap dealers for 2 cents a pound, but an ounce of VM turned out to be worth 10 million pounds of scrap. Purchasing Supervisor Jim Voelkel contacted local reconditioners to see if they wanted to enter into a joint venture—you fix, you sell, we split the profits 50/50. Thanks to his VM variation, Amoco saves $200,000 a year, What was "junk" has been redefined as being "saleable," and an altered character has created a profitable alter ego.

13. SUBSTITUTE/INTERCHANGE or 14. STABILIZE. VM often provides multiple benefits from a single change. At Philadelphia Gear Corporation, for example, the company switched from a water-based mineral oil coolant to a semi-synthetic compound. The second compound was more stable (the former had problems with rancidity), lowered maintenance costs, and increased useful coolant life from two to six weeks (on some operations, the lifeline increased to as long as seven months). Philadelphia Gear saved over $50,000 in the first year alone.

15. REVERSE. Does the left hand know what the right hand is doing? Commonalities can lead to handsome benefits. Joy Manufacturing VMers found that both right-hand and left-hand bearing housing-supports could use the same model plate. A simple reverse met both needs. By producing a single component, Joy cut total housing subassembly costs by 33%. How's that for reverse psychology?

16. UPGRADE/REPLACE. Boeing replaced a vacuum tube in its B-52 with solid-state technology and saved $2,000 per unit while increasing product reliability. First year total savings were estimated at $350,000. Boeing has long been a big believer in VM. Malcolm Stamper, Boeing President, says, "Everybody at Boeing is responsible for increasing the quality of the product, improving productivity, and working 'smarter.' That is where the leverage is, and this is why Boeing can be optimistic about its future."

17. INCREASE RESILIENCE. When the going gets tough, the tough get Value Management. Skil Corporation replaced the aluminum pulley wheels in its tabletop bandsaws with a thermoplastic unit. Increase dimensional stability allows the material to withstand tremendous compression. The "replacement part" meets all necessary functions (heat deflection, warp resistance, etc.) and offers an estimated 50% savings on finishing costs. That's a Skil-ful example of functional thinking.

18. STANDARDIZE/MAKE UNIFORM. By using a standardized label printing system, Sheller-Globe's electric motor plant (Gainesville, GA) customized a series of savings. The company was able to cut the number of label formats from 150 to four, do in-house sourcing for printing/labels, and add date coding. Sheller-Globe also cut the cost of printed labels from between 25 to 30 cents apiece to 9 and 10 cents. Total annual savings: $30,000 and 250 manhours. The payback was less than one year. This VM project was labeled an unequivocal success.

19. MAKE THE PRODUCT MORE EXPENSIVE OR CHEAPER. Who would have thought that adding a simple label (albeit an embroidered Vanderbilt or Calvin Klein) to a pair of blue jeans would quadruple its market value/

price? Twenty years ago, the Perrier program would have seemed all wet. Today, that annual market is in the millions (hardly a drop in the bucket). Even pet rocks rocketed to momentary success.

20. ADD/CHANGE/SUBTRACT COLOR. A range hood manufactured by Philips Industries contained black, white, and red wiring. The white wire was the ground, the red wire represented heat, and the black wire was the cheapest. Philips continued to color-code long after the hood was redesigned and the need for ground and hot coding was eliminated. After a VM study, all wiring was changed to basic black. This is the kind of simple VM recommendation that helps keep a company out of the red.

Can we improve the quality/cost/value of the subject by changing product/component conditions? Can we make the product:

21. HOT/COLD. Unnecessary manufacturing costs get a cold shoulder at Stanley Tools. The firm cut one product's manufacturing cost approximately 25% by specifying a cold-heading production process on a magnetic-tip screwdriver shaft. The new process, a one-step operation, eliminated the need for drilling and broaching the hex socket. No wonder more and more companies are warming up to the idea of Value Management!

22. INCORPORATE OPEN/CLOSE. Initially, Pet met the "open/close" functions of its Accent canister with an unreliable three-component cover (underdisc, turn disc, dust cover). With help from suppliers (Blue Water Engineering in Grand Prairie, TX, and Conpack South in Marion, AL), Pet replaced the triple threat with a one-piece injection molded part. The company saves 10% per year on cover costs and market testing verified consumer preference for the new design (Fig. 6-2).

Like many VM studies, this Pet project resulted in a patentable idea. For years, the top 100 corporations receiving patents have included a disproportionate number of value-inspired champions. In 1984, four of the top five patent receivers (GE with 785, IBM with 608, Hitachi Ltd. with 596, and U.S. Philips Corporation with 438) were value practitioners.

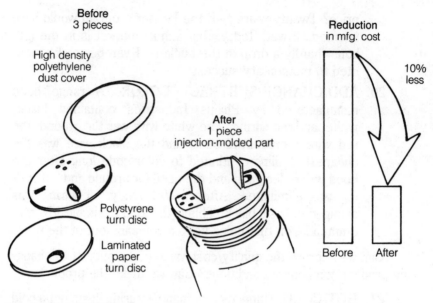

Fig. 6-2. Pet VM Project.

23. **PREFORM, 24. INCORPORATE, 25. LUBRICATE.**
TRW was able to combine all three of these conditional improvements in a new VMed shifter lever that it sells to the major truck builder, Freightliner (another big VM user). The aluminum extrusion pillow block was replaced by Deldrin, a molded plastic. The mold incorporated necessary holes, a preform function that saved on drilling costs. Since Deldrin is self-lubricating, bearing costs were eliminated. The score: aluminum pillow block—$4.40 per unit; Deldrin—$1.44 a piece.

26. **DISPOSE/REUSE.** VM ideas don't have to be earth-shattering to be cost-battering. By rebuilding rather than "refuse-ing" old forklift truck batteries, the Budd Company saves around $2,625 per battery. Senior Buyer Richard LaFeir, the value victor, gets a real charge out of that.

27. **SEPARATE/PART.** A VM study conducted by Consulting Value Specialists Incorporated found that three helipad storage areas would never need access to a main airport

facility. By keeping the separate facilities separate (e.g., eliminating a proposed infrastructure that would connect two areas), CVS saved project owners over $1 million.

28. SOLIDIFY/LIQUEFY. Byrd Laboratories sells dehydrated drug-free humane urine to people worried about drug tests. While some might argue that this is taking the concept of "liquid assets" a bit too far, Byrd's business is whizzing right along.

29. PULVERIZE. The Ford Motor Company replaced an automotive air conditioner's nodular casting swash plate with a pulverized P/M (powder metallurgy) unit. This prototype project is an excellent example of why VM requires in-depth examinations. The P/M blanks cost 50% more than Ford's nodular casting. In nonVM surface studies, that would eliminate the product from future consideration, but VM doesn't make decisions based on a single piece of data. While the P/M blank is more expensive, that cost is offset by reduced labor costs and increased productivity. Using the P/M process, Ford drove home a 7% reduction in manufacturing costs and a 50% increase in the part production rate.

30. PREVENT/PROMOTE/WITHSTAND A WET OR DRY CONDITION. Even product designers who are still wet behind the ears know that moisture condensation can create costly problems. The City of Philadelphia saved an estimated life cycle cost of $344,000 on a composting facility by replacing a steel-framed roof with a precast, pre-stressed concrete roofing system that would better withstand continual moisture. The City of Brotherly Love also loves to save a buck.

31. ELASTICIZE. Sometimes, VM has to stretch to make a point—or a profit. General Electric once used a $4.75 castellated nut to hold a high-temperature part to a vibrating shaft. By changing to a specially-designed elastic stopnut, the firm cut unit costs to 23 cents and eliminated the need for drilling and wiring. Certainly, one doesn't have to stretch the truth to call a 95% cost reduction significant (Fig. 6-3).

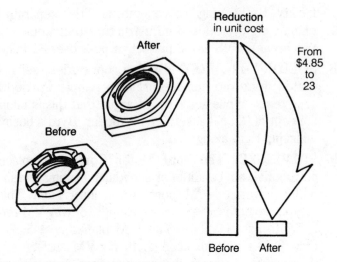

Fig. 6-3. GE castellated nut and hi-temp nut.

32. INCREASE RESISTANCE. One major environmental hazard is the business regulatory environment. When Custodis-Hamon Constructors (Everett, WA) made required improvements to its 275-foot kraft pulp mill chimney, pH levels fell from 6 to 1.5 and the chimney lining started to falter. Through VM, the company identified a closed cellular foamed borosilicate inorganic material that could replace the chimney's FRP/brick liner. Fourteen months after insulation, the lining was inspected and there was no cracking, thermal, or chemical damage.

33. CENTRALIZE/DECENTRALIZE. It isn't easy to keep track of 30,000 different parts, but in no small part, VM was responsible for helping the Universal Sewing Supply Company (St. Louis, MO) to simplify its inventory operations. By changing from a decentralized to a centralized storage system (one which creatively crunched 6,000 square feet of storage space into 2,000 square feet of floor space), Value Management cut error rates on order selections by over 85%, reduced returns for credit by 50%, and slashed labor costs by 30%.

34. INCREASE OR DECREASE SPEED. By redesigning and speeding up its corrugated material strapping system, St. Regis Paper doubled productivity while cutting labor and material costs. The company originally moved bulk

material from the corrugator to a second strapping and shipment area. Under its new directive, corrugated caseloads run off the corrugator into the arms of a semiautomatic strapper. With its new system up to speed, St. Regis anticipates a speedy payback.

35. CHANGE DIRECTION. The scenic route is fine for travelling but lousy for planning. VM often finds projects that ignore the "path of least resistance" in favor of the "path of longest resistance." For example, CVS Incorporated once saved a client $200,000 by changing the direction of a proposed power cable and accessing a closer power source. By digging on the left (rather than the right) side of his building, the project owner didn't have to dig quite so far into his pockets.

Can we improve the quality/cost/value of the subject by changing the form of the product/component? Can we:

36. ELIMINATE SOMETHING or 37. ADD SOMETHING. Are you throwing money away? You may be, thanks to a traditional design throwback. General Dynamic's VM team evaluated a hydraulic valve on the F-16 jet fighter and found that it served no useful function (e.g., new designs made its function redundant). Removing the valve saved $600,000 and cut maintenance time. The moral of the story: It's always better to save money for today's sake than to keep a relic for old-time's sake.

In the same vein, another VM recommendation on the F-16 was to add a spacer on the brake mechanism. The modified design increased brake life from 700 hours to 1,229 hours and saved $38.3 million on labor and materials.

38. COMBINE SOMETHING. AM International combined a separate motor and vacuum pump assembly into a single unit. This cut unit costs on the 1330/1360 duplicator product line by $37.73 per machine (this same change offered varying reductions on three other product lines). This particular VM improvement was important to AMI because the 1330/1360 series was the highest volume product in the company's master schedule. This only goes to show that even a winner has room for VM improvement.

39. COPY COMPETITORS or 40. USE INDUSTRY STANDARDS. When a company is "odd man out" in terms of product design or costs, the odds are good that it should reexamine competitive/industry standards. Eaton's Controls Division used a magnetic wire with a very thick polyurethane coating. In fact, the coating was twice as thick as the industry standard. No competitors used a similar wire (which in the trade became known as "Eaton wire"). Through VM, corporate questioner Robert Hansen found that the wire was overspecified. A switch to standard magnetic wire now saves the company more than $250,000 annually.

41. SIMPLIFY. The KISS chorus (Keep It Simple, Stupid!) is a vital VM verse. Bell & Howell's bulk-mail inserting machine used to include a 57-part hub (one stamping blank, eight specialized parts, 16 sets of cap screws, nuts, lockwashers, etc.). The B&H vendor (Dayton Rogers Manufacturing) suggested a one-piece stamped design that reduced unit costs by $9.60. Bell & Howell also saved on maintenance (there were 56 fewer parts to come loose!), repair costs (hub replacement was cheap and easy), inventory, and administrative costs.

42. PROVIDE/GIVE UP PROXIMITY OR FAST TRANSMIT. Operation Eagle was launched by Boeing as an aggressive cost control/quality drive. Boeing Vertol (Philadelphia, PA) employee Dan McKeown saved the firm $464,000 by freeing up channels for parts interchanges between different models of Chinook helicopters. That same year, Boeing save $579 million via VM-type programs and passed on an additional $140 million in savings to the Department of Defense. Their Operation Eagle/VM efforts are flying high.

43. CHANGE/CONFORM TO CONTOURS. A careful VM inspection will show many companies that their products are out of shape. For example, when St. Regis redesigned the packaging for a printed-circuit board manufacturer, it replaced polystyrene packing "peanuts" with a simple die-cut insert. This literally suspended the circuit boards within each box and prevented the product from hitting

the side walls of the corrugated box and sustaining damage. As a result, a 42% damage rate was reduced to nearly zero. Obviously, VM can change the shape of things to come.

44. CHANGE THE SHAPE (MAKE REGULAR/IRREGULAR/SYMMETRICAL/CURVED/STRAIGHT/ETC.). Joy Manufacturing replaced a two-part (one horizontal, one vertical) brake pedal component with a single piece of bent metal. This reduced unit costs from $5.04 to $1.52 and cut the number of manufacturing steps from six to three. According to Art Mudge, it also reduced the work load in the machine and structural shops, warehouse, material control department, materials handling division, and accounting (Fig. 6-4).

45. MAKE A COMPONENT HARDER OR SOFTER. Taking a hard look at product components can lead to a softening of standards. Sikorsky Aircraft Division (Stratford, CT) was having assembly problems on its H-60 combat helicopter control unit. Sikorsky specified aluminum for components because of the material's light weight. Unfortunately, a U-shaped bracket proved too soft for its function (it didn't offer sufficient thread strength when tapped)

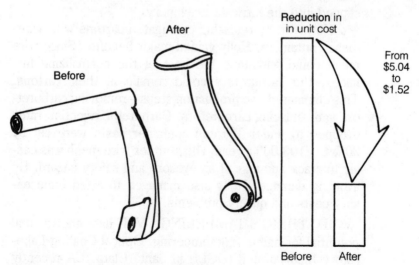

Fig. 6-4. Joy Manufacturing brake pedal.

and material weakness limited the component to one-side access. Sikorsky replaced the bracket with a Penn Engineering and Manufacturing (Danboro, PA) self-clinching fastener. The component offers more reliability and strength as well as better access.

46. **ADD NOTCHES** or 47. **CHANGE THE SURFACE FINISH (ROUGHER/SMOOTHER/ETC.).** Sometimes, VM is a sight for sore eyes. An Austin, TX program for visually impaired Americans is providing banks with on-site Braille instruction plaques for their ATMs (automatic transfer machines). A one-time total cost of $4 to $10 allows any bank to increase account access for thousands of people. It doesn't take 20/20 vision to see that VM can substantially increase product/service value without significantly increasing product/service cost.

48. **AVOID DAMAGE/ACCIDENTS.** Holly carburetor "bodies" were entombed in corrugated cartons, and were not allowed to rest in peace. The units were removed from the cartons and heated in the normalizing furnace, replaced in the boxes, moved to the machining area for casting work, replaced in the cartons, moved to the testing areas, and so on. The boxes were taking a beating—and so was product quality. As the boxes decomposed, cardboard particles slipped into the intricate machinery.

However, by replacing corrugated cartons with wire-mesh containers, Holly gained major benefits. Since wire mesh could withstand the heat of the normalizing furnaces, the carburetors could remain in their cartons. This eliminated two production steps—removing carburetors and replacing carburetors. Carburetor rejection rates dropped to under 1% and container costs were cut by 20% to $100,000 a year. The sturdier wire mesh was easier to stack and less of an eyesore and safety hazard. By avoiding damage, Holly also managed to avoid unnecessary costs and quality problems.

49. **AVOID THEFTS/TAMPERING.** VM has shown real potential for hampering tampering. Optical Coating Laboratory Incorporated (OCLI) in Santa Clara, CA recently developed a packing material that changes color under

physical stress. Antitampering lids on foods, medicines, etc., change from a bright color to a dull gray once the opening label has been peeled back and stretched. At a cost of less than two cents per package, this offers a reliable and cost-effective functional alternative for concerned consumer companies.

50. AVOID/BENEFIT FROM DELAYS. JIT inventory management is an obvious example of functional fiddling. Another example comes from Dataproducts in Woodland Hills, CA. Buyer Jean Connell found that streamlined transportation procedures and a carefully monitored use of slow-but-reliable sea freight (vs. fast forward airlifts) cut the company's freight burden rate (total freight cost divided by total value of shipped goods) by 34%. VM can help a company determine when money should save time, or when time should save money.

The ideas that generated these spectacular scenarios are clearly creative, *but the Creative Phase is not a good/better/best test.* For example, this is not the time for Value teams to decide that the *best* way to connect materials is by using only one of the following:

a) Glue

b) Tongue-and-groove designs

c) Mechanical fasteners

d) Welding

The function of the creation phase is to *identify as many ways* to connect materials as possible. The creation corps needs to play the numbers. It might start by suggesting:

a) Glue

b) Tongue-and-groove designs

c) Mechanical fasteners

d) Welding

e) Nuts/bolts

f) Interlocking materials

g) Buttons

    h) Laminants

    i) Snaps

    j) Magnets—plus . . .

and as many other answers as the team can suggest. In the Creative Phase, VM goes for *quantity*, not *quality*. As we'll soon see, mixing creation with justification creates obfuscation.

7

The Evaluation Phase

AT THIS POINT IN THE VALUE MANAGEMENT STUDY, EVEN THE MOST
vigilant VMer may feel caught in a terminal loop. It's like finally
reaching the end of the song *One Thousand Bottles of Beer On the
Wall* and having a perky voice from the back of the schoolbus chirp,
"One more time!"

That's because, even though we call this phase "evaluation,"
we again *focus on function*. Why the functional refrain? Because if
our alternative answers don't fulfill the functions in question, they
are of less-than-questionable value. Because a focus on function
nullifies the natural tendency to cheapen a product via cost or quality. (NOTE: Eliminating unnecessary functions doesn't cheapen a
product—it improves it.) Because the functional framework stops a
team from maintaining the mediocre "just because."

Actually, the Evaluation Phase could easily be renamed
the "Recreative Phase." Ideas from the Creative Phase are
reworked—refined, combined, confined, or left behind—using four
appraisal/judgment techniques. The VM team's creative fluff is
spun into closely knit functional alternatives. At this point, members will develop only a *working* wardrobe of function-fitting ideas;
ornamental *sell* functions will be applied to the product/system
later on.

Now, let's examine the four steps of this phase.

STEP 1: The Take-Its-Measure Mandate

Here, the VM team studies its brainstorming by-products. Every creative idea is analyzed to determine its advantages and disadvantages. Whether a component's associated attributes (strength, weight, density, size, condition, availability, speed, high or low quality, form, shape, layout, track record, etc.) are advantages or disadvantages depend on its functional fit.

The team then cashes in on its creative cache by identifying ways to:

- *Augment* a given idea's advantages or disarm it disadvantages;
- *Combine* ideas to offset disadvantages and synthesize or optomize advantages; and/or
- *Change* or *rearrange* an idea to sharpen its functional fine points.

Ansul's Value Management team used all three of these techniques when brainstorming its fire extinguisher. For example, VMers *augmented* the idea of standardized inspection tags by standardizing them to the paper—rather than the liner cloth—model. This saved 16% on inspection tag costs.

Ansul *combined* its product manual with the warranty card and switched to a lighter paper, which cut printing costs in half. Ansul combined four extinguisher parts into one, saving $90,000 annually (Fig. 7-1).

Ansul *changed* its approach to the "hang extinguisher" function. By replacing a big bracket with a simple hanger hook, the company saved 10% on component costs (Fig. 7-2). For the final tally, Ansul was able to cut the distribution price on the improved extinguisher from $15.20 to $11.75. A company can do wonderful things when it's fired up about VM!

Throughout the refine/combine/confine/leave behind basics, each team member must keep two critical concerns in mind. First, will this alternative be able to provide all of its necessary functions? Second, if we choose this alternative, how will it affect the fulfillment of other related functions?

A VM team might suggest replacing an expensive alloy with aluminum, but would have to determine if aluminum meets *all* of the required material functions (strength, hardness, wear resistance, workability, etc.), not just the "primary" concerns. Then,

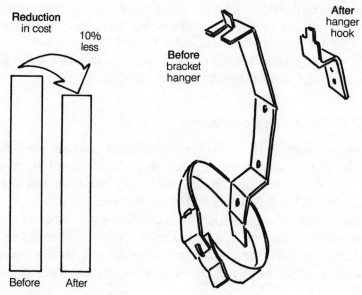

Fig. 7-1. Ansul bracket/hanger.

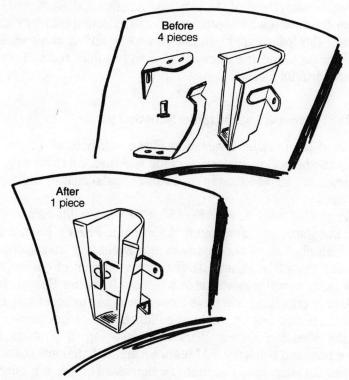

Fig. 7-2. Ansul will save over $90,000/yr. on this one part.

if the material fulfills its own functions, its effect on other components has to be effectively evaluated. For example, would aluminum's lighter weight affect the unit's balance?

It's a tough task, but the take-its-measure mandate is the first
measured step toward improved costs and quality.

STEP 2: The Cash Register

The second step of the evaluative consultation is where costs first
begin to register as a concern. They *do* register—about 10 on the
Richter scale. Costs are crucial. After all, when we talk about
change, we're not talking about pocket change.

Each idea, or combination of ideas, needs a reasonably accurate estimated cost; the VM team requires a based-in-reality reck-
oning. At this point, vendors, purchasing agents, trade catalogs/
publications/advertisements, etc., give a good-enough guessti-
mate.

Why the sudden cost craze, and why now? No VM team can
thoroughly analyze all of the available functional alternatives. Taking the cost-conscious approach—that is, starting in-depth analy-
ses with the least expensive creative ideas and working up from
there—helps prune the decision tree and to limit team efforts to
the most fruitful foliage.

STEP 3: Structuring Suitable Substitutes

The third level of the Evaluation Phase is where all of the VM
team's methodical meanderings come together. All roads may lead
to Rome, but all VM roamin' eventually leads back to the area of
functions.

The VM team has gathered all necessary information/data
about the status quo component (Information Phase). Its members
have identified all of the component's necessary and secondary
functions (Function Phase). It also has a quorum of quality ideas
ready to be woven into workable whatnots (Creative Phase). Now,
the team's principle problem is to weed out any unnecessary costs
and to fertilize a few favorable—and functional!—fabrications.

The Function Format Worksheet (see Fig. 5-1) starts from
square one, and helps the VM team square its functional goals with
its potential solutions. The first function listed on the worksheet is
the function with the highest weight. The lowest-cost creative

alternative for fulfilling that function is listed to its right. The second function listed is the function with the second highest weight. The creative idea tied to this second stringer is the alternative which works best with the first functional alternative at the lowest cost. The third function listed is the function with the third highest weight, and the creative idea tied to it is the alternative which works best with the first and second functional alternatives at the lowest cost. This same process is repeated until the VM team has listed all necessary functions. The result? One formidable form.

The VM team needs to build a series of Function Format Worksheets using different creative alternatives (e.g., using the second-string alternative to meet the primary function, then the best matching alternative to fulfill the second function. The more structured options a VM team has, the more likely it is to find a really viable one.[1]

This is not an empty-headed exercise in filling forms. VM team members should simultaneously create, develop, question, evaluate, investigate, and implement any late-blooming alternatives to its "initial" alternatives. Creation doesn't appear in one VM phase, only to disappear in another; rather, VM continually teams up with creativity.

Now that the VM team has identified several suitable substitutes with a functional fit, it's time to identify the superior suit.

STEP 4: Compare and Contrast

The basic function of the Evaluation Phase is to turn a large pool of creative ideas into a more manageable, more meaningful puddle. In this step, a VM team determines which of its alternatives are all wet.

Each of the options documented on a Function Format Worksheet needs to be assessed in terms of its advantages and disadvantages. Every last plus and minus should be accounted for. The evaluation then begins in earnest.

How do the advantages compare to the disadvantages? Are they about even, or is one area stronger? What are the trade-offs? Can a disadvantage be approached as a new (but solvable) problem? Would a new approach change the disadvantage into an advantage? Do the advantages of a given option suggest an acceptable

---

[1]Though VM's methodical methods minimize risk, risk is *inherent* in any change. However, the decision *not* to change (e.g. grow) also involves a certain amount of risk.

payback? In other words, will the improvement in costs, productivity, functionality, reliability, maintainability, repairability, quality, saleability, accessibility, etc., justify all changeover costs?

Consider the change that Ansul made in its extinguisher levers and handles. VMers considered replacing the painted steel pieces with an unpainted aluminum option. Steel's advantage and disadvantage, respectively, were material strength and cost (material and painting labor). Conversely, aluminum shone in the cost department and was weak in the strength section.

For this component, decreased costs were the powerful plus. The strength trade-off—the disadvantage—could be solved by using heavier gauge aluminum. The change was not difficult to make, and the payoff was more than acceptable. Ansul's handle/lever costs were reduced by 40% (Fig. 7-3).

After all options have been assessed, they need to be reassessed relative to the other possibilities. Is Option 1 better than Option 2? How much better? In what ways is it better/worse? In what ways are the options similar? In what ways are they different? Can the team make good on the best of both options and disperse the down-side disadvantages?

Ansul had the option of maintaining its current how-to instructional nameplate (which required two pressure sensitive labels) or

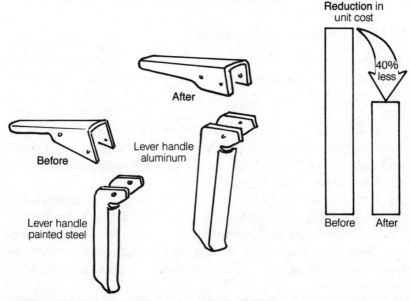

Fig. 7-3. Ansul handle/lever.

reducing the component to a single label. Did Option 1 meet the "inform user" function more effectively than Option 2? No. Ansul took its alternate idea to an outside ad agency where it got expert assistance in meeting the inform function. In what ways were the options similar or different? Same basic information, different sizes. The ad agency helped condense the text and graphics so that they fit on one smaller label.

Was Option 2 better? Yes. How was it better? This option presented the information in a more concise format, definitely useful in "crisis management." How much was it better? Option 2 met all of the required functions—and cut nameplate costs by 47%.

The amount of creative crunching necessary depends on the complexity of the project and the options available. Once the VM team is comfortable with its options, they should be ranked according to their comparative strengths and benefits. The team and its alternatives are then ready for the final test—the in-depth Investigation Phase.

Like many steaks, the Evaluation Phase is tougher than it looks, but the payoff isn't tough to understand. The best creative ideas in the world are *useless* unless they are put into play, and this phase plays with component combinations until it identifies the most tractable teams.

8

The Investigation Phase

WHAT YOU DON'T KNOW CAN HURT YOU. CONSIDER THE CASE OF "planned economy." In the mid-1970s, the Nigerian government decided to modernize. Government planners ordered approximately 20 million tons of cement to build an infrastructure as per its Third National Nigerian Development Plan. All cement—fully one-third of the world's supply—was to be shipped to the Lagos docks, thereby "cementing" the country's place in history.

Unfortunately, the planners had not investigated all of the project's weighty concerns. The Lagos docks were only large enough to unload 2,000 tons of cement a day (at one point, 27 years worth of "work" was anchored off the port). The unsettling conclusion? The cement fulfilled it's settling function—mostly in the cargo holds of waiting freighters.

The moral of the story is that it doesn't take much research to weigh down a project; it only takes less than needed.

The Investigation Phase of Value Management is a room with a *déjà vu* view. It has the same basis of acquisition as that of the information phase. In both phases, the VM team's major goal is to gather relevant data. The only difference is that new alternatives are studied in this phase.

At this point in the VM study, the team has solid options for improvement. The question now is: which single option will fulfill all necessary functions at a low(er) cost, with improved quality, increased productivity, etc.? Again, the team turns to some guidelines.

GUIDELINE 1: Check Out Company/Industrial Standards

The use of standards (parts, processes, products, concepts, tolerances, materials, etc.) offers some pretty standard benefits (make that *very* pretty). Replacing a pain-in-the-neck special with a run-of-the-mill standard can lift a major millstone off a company's neck. Standards don't involve developmental costs, retooling costs, patent problems, a long purchasing lead time, monopolistic suppliers, regulatory approval problems, and so on. In addition, a standard's track record in terms of overall costs, quality, reliability, performance characteristics, etc., are all easy to track down; the trial-and-error phase of development has already taken place in somebody else's competitive courtroom.

Eaton's Hydraulic Division (Shawnee, OK) stipulated a special proprietary[1] steel when its product specifications were first written in 1973. Times had changed, but the specs hadn't kept up with them. After intense investigation, Sung Cho (a new Senior Buyer responsible for commodity purchases) found that he could substitute standard stock and save Eaton at least $250,000 a year.

It is important to remember, however, that standards can function as a friend or foe. If a VM team uses the standard because its effect on overall cost, quality, productivity, etc., is positive—then *hurray!* If the team tries to use a standard simply because it exists, or the team is biased/lazy, or the standard looks cheaper (cheaper component costs but higher overall costs)—then *no way*. According to Art Mudge, "Standards are like roads. Whether they work for or against the Value team is a matter of group skill. Traditional inroads can either be used to take the team where it wants to go or to keep its members on the beaten path."

GUIDELINE 2: Check into "Specials"

Specials also offer a bevy of benefits. New and improved processes, components, materials, etc., can often meet old functions at a lower cost or offer a higher quality product. Designing specials may make it possible to add desired functions or to create totally

---

[1]Check anything specified "proprietary." The designation probably does more for the vendor than it does for the buyer.

new ones. A special can often circumvent standard product problems.

A "new" special can even be tried-and-true. A process or material that is old hat in one industry may be a hats-off innovation to another. In this case, the special would also feature a track record.

A "special" example involves Douglas Pedder of Lightolier (Fall River, MA). UL wiring standards required the company to use SF-1 wire (covered with silicone and a fiberglass jacket) in its track lighting systems. Under standard operating procedures, that meant two ugly wires running from fixture to socket. Aesthetically, a tacky tracky. So, Lightolier workers had to cover the two wires with a single fiberglass sleeve and tape both ends. This was high-cost work.

Pedder convinced vendors to develop a special one-piece, two-conductor cable that met UL standards and his product needs. The result? Lightolier saves approximately $50,000 annually (the new molded cable costs 18 cents per foot compared to 26 cents per assembled foot on the old style) and, thanks to the product's improved aesthetics, the firm was able to increase its market share.

Warning! When diving into special-interest areas, the VM team needs to investigate the subject in depth. Advertising and marketing claims need to be verified. The team must separate the "guaranteed" from the "snare-unteed."[2] Only fully developed proccesses, materials, etc., should be considered. VM teams should "smell a rat" prior to becoming a vendor's "laboratory rat."

In short, being a "standard" or a "special" doesn't ensure VM approval; it only ensures VM consideration.

GUIDELINE 3: Check with the Experts

How does the VM team determine if a standard or a special offers the superior deal? It goes back to the experts—the same experts accessed in the Information Phase—to get the goods (or the bads, as the case may be) on a given option.

The team will pow-wow with internal chiefs and Indians alike. Team members will ask for function-aimed feedback. Will this component meet this need? Is there a substitute component (lower cost, higher quality, etc.) that could be made to fulfill this function?

---

[2]It might help to remember McGowan's Madison Avenue Axiom: If an item is advertised as "under $50," you can bet it's not $19.95.

Who else can give us relevant feedback? Are there any company standards we could apply to the option that would augment an alternative's advantages or dispense its disadvantages?

The VM team will tend to current and/or potential vendors. It will ask the same kinds of questions it asked the corporate corps. Will this component meet this need? Do you know of a substitute component (lower cost, high quality, etc.) that could be made to fulfill this function? Can your product designers, researchers, client references, etc., provide any relevant feedback? Do you have any company standards we could apply to the option that would augment an alternative's advantages or dispense it disadvantages? How much would this option cost (and under what purchasing conditions)?

Again, vendors can be found by talking to company purchasing agents, in specialty indexes, (*Thomas Register of American Manufacturers*, *Industrial Arts Index*), reading subject magazines and/or newsletters (*Ulrich's International Periodicals Directory* lists over 40,000 specialty magazines; the *National Directory of Newsletters and Reporting Services* is the best reference work for its major medium), etc.

Industrial experts can be located through trade and/or professional and/or research associations (Gale's *Encyclopedia of Associations* lists thousands of associations by subject/key word), dissertation location services (*American Doctoral Dissertations*, *Dissertation Abstracts International*, etc.), or by browsing through special library collections (*Directory of Special Libraries and Information Centers*). Most of these reference works are available at either public or university libraries.

At this point, the VM team also needs to get the goods about its goods from the consumer. The team already knows that proposed product alternatives meet all of the customers' work needs. That's the reason for its function focus. However, only the customer can tell the VM team what will make the product sell. Consumer research is time-consuming, but it also devours potential marketing mistakes.[3]

Once upon a time, Ford Motor Company "had a better idea," or so it thought. The company designed a car "perfectly geared to

---

[3]In many cases, a VM team will be trying to sell its "product" (change) to corporate managers. The issue then is, "What will it take to convince the decision-makers to buy into our VM program?"

American taste''—the Edsel—but customers wouldn't bite. The Edsel went out of production in a mere two years, two months and 15 days and $350 million short of Ford's break-even point.

Quoting one successful Certified Value Specialist, ''The choice is clear: expert check or project wreck.''

GUIDELINE 4: Garbage In, Garbage Out

To paraphrase an old cliche, ''As you show so shall you reap.'' The VM team needs to share its information with all interested experts if it wants meaningful feedback. For example, a vendor needs to know the required functions of a product so as to come up with functional alternatives (vs. replace one product with another). Any expert needs a functional frame of reference in which to frame relevant VM responses. In particular, the VM team must share the goal of its project: to provide a specific high-quality function at the lowest possible overall cost.

When Randy Hyde of Skil Corporation approached applications specialist Gary Lee of Camcar (Taptite Division, Rockford, IL) about replacing the traditional fasteners of a power tool motor's casing with plastic thread-forming screws, he passed on all the functional information needed for evaluation. Working together, the two cut Skil's fastening costs by $78,000 a year and eliminated two product assembly stations.

GUIDELINE 5: Time Out

In Value Management, time is not of the essence—it is of the essential. Even the best laid plans of mice and men can be waylaid. What chance does a project have when its progenitors fail to do their homework? In-depth investigations take energy, enthusiasm, effort,—and time. Unfortunately, few planners take the present time or the current trouble necessary to avoid future problems.

Many people are more concerned with time than professionalism. London's Dr. Robert Liston (reputed in his time to be the ''fastest knife in the West End'') provides ample evidence of the proverb ''haste makes waste.'' He is chiefly remembered for one operating-table record. In the early 1840s, he amputated a patient's leg in two-and-a-half minutes (the patient later died of gangrene in a hospital). At the same time, his overly enthusiastic swipe took off three of his young assistant's fingers (the boy also died of gangrene) and ripped the coattails of a surgical spectator (who was so frightened by the "knifing" that he died of a heart attack). The record: two-and-a-half minutes flat, three people flat.

A speedy investigative phase won't kill VM, but it will injure project outcome. Value Management benefits can last for years. An important project is worth a timely down payment.

Investigative work may seem like make work. It's actually "keeping the team from making a mistake" work. A solid investigation of project alternatives is what keeps VM's "best laid plans" from laying an egg. Unless, of course, the egg in question is the proverbial "golden egg."

9

The Recommendation/ Implementation Phase

IN THE STRICTEST SEMANTIC SENSE, THE VM PROJECT IS NOW complete (e.g., the team has identified a better product/service with a lower cost). Still, now that the actual *VM* work is done, the *real* work begins.

Over the last five project phases, the VM team focused on the work and/or sell functions of a specific product/service. Now, the team again focuses on work and sell functions, but this time the functions are team functions. The team needs to "work" and to "sell"; that is, the VMers need to work on sales strategies that will help sell top management on their project recommendations.

Up to this point, Value Management has been an all-for-one affair. All relevant parties have participated, and all team members have teamworked, towards one goal: improving a product/service. The VMers have thoroughly studied an item's necessary functions, status quo design, and appreciably better alternatives. They probably see the chance to provide a much better product at a far lower cost.

It is said, "There are none so blind as those who will not see." It is also true that there are none so blinded to human nature as those who think we all see in the same way. A corporate manager, for example, is likely to see the VM recommendations differently than the team players do. After all, he hasn't had the benefit of weeks or months of agonizing on-the-spot analysis.

The manager responsible for accepting or rejecting a given idea is being asked to replace "one of our own" with a "lesser known." He may respond with the old adage, "If it ain't broke, don't fix [or improve] it." Many managers are asked to accept VM recommendations that completely reject a product's past design premise. Some managers have a low tolerance level for high-level technology.[1] These are just a few of the reasons for one of the strangest physical phenomena of Value Management. When the VM team *says* "positive change, improvements, benefits," management often *hears* "risk, risk, risk." The VM and management perspectives are parsecs apart.

That's why most VM studies separate proposed savings from accepted savings. Management often accepts only a small portion of a project's recommended improvements. For example, when a group of CVSs undertook an open-ended value contract with the Sacramento District of the U.S. Air Force, consultants had accepted savings of $3,869,973—a cost-to-savings ratio of 1:65.2. However, $9,535,466 in savings was proposed—a ratio of 1:206.8.

At the bottom line, VM teams have the power to investigate, but not dictate, change. The approval of recommendations is a boss's business. VM teams can't drag management kicking and screaming toward competitiveness; conversely, a manager *can* scream at suggestions and have the VMers kicked out of his office. Therefore, salesmanship is required to turn VM recommendations into VM implementations.[2]

The Recommendation/Implementation Phase is a two-step process. The first is that of recommendation justification, and the second step is that of implementation intimation.

To begin the recommendation justification, the VM team needs to devise a "who will see?" strategy. Which manager(s) will approve or disapprove of these recommendations? Does he like a great deal of detail or is detail no big deal? Is he open to change or closed to new ideas? Is he more interested in cost or quality? Is he a gung ho decision-maker or a go slow time-taker? In short, how can the team facilitate a "yes" response?

---

[1]At Ampex (a one-time leader in VCR base technology), vacuum tube-tied managers reportedly had signs on their desks that said "Stamp out transistors".

[2]For the Principles of Salesmanship beyond the Principles of VM, consult The Whole Sale Bibliography at the end of this chapter.

Once the team has a good make on the decision-maker(s), it can develop the print/picture project presentation. Most groups devise a short-and-sweet, exhort-the-feat summary that tells management everything it needs to know before making a decision, specifically: before and after item attributes (problems, opportunities, improvements, etc.), before and after costs (including present costs, recommended costs, implemented costs, expected savings), relevant before and after the facts, and reasoned responses.

Before and after attributes quantify the need for action (we have a major problem that has to be solved, we are letting an important opportunity get away, etc.). Management doesn't have to be sold on VM's recommendations to be sold on VM's instigations.

Take, for example, the case of the sluggish supplier. Emcee Broadcast Products (White Haven, PA) had chronic problems with a terminally late vendor of heat sink sources. To make matters worse, the supplier announced even longer lag times. It didn't take VM to convince management that there was a problem. Still, it did take VM to *solve* the problem. By finding a new vendor and purchasing a more finished product, Ron Rapczynski and his VM team were able to cut the parts and labor cost of the component from $104.88 each to $31.71.

A solid summary of costs is crucial because it proves to the decision-maker(s) that the VM team studied the cost question under accountants' shades rather than through rose-colored glasses. While present costs can and must be accurate, recommended and implemented costs should be over-estimated and expected savings should be under-estimated. What VM can't pledge, it must hedge. After all, suppliers or delivery companies can raise costs, etc. VM promotes cost conservation in lieu of verification.

Harry Durkin's VM team at General Binding Corporation (Northbrook, IL) found that a redesigned resistor roll would cut unit costs from $28 to $15 (saving the company $90,000 annually). Cost reductions of 45% are impressive, but so are 35% or 30% improvements. A VM team can report lower than anticipated savings to be sure that any management "surprises" are good ones.

Facts are critical because they elicit the "yes" response. Decision-makers can't argue with an objective, verifiable, relevant fact. The VM summary should present a solid fact attack. The more a manager settles down into the "yes" response ("Yes, I agree with that fact, and that fact, and that fact . . . ."), the harder it is to up and say no" ("I agree with everything you say but not with you!"). In short, when VMers cement one relevant fact upon another, they lay a solid foundation for conclusion fusion.

Ever since OPEC's heavy-handed oil embargo, RV manufacturers have tried to lighten their products. Aluminum quickly replaced steel because of one simple fact: aluminum weighs less. However, as smart VMers know, the facts don't always speak for themselves or tell the whole truth.

A VM study led by Phillip Geise of Holiday Rambler Corporation (Wakaruse, IN) found that the aluminum tubing in one model's deck area could be replaced with a thinner gauge steel. The important facts of the matter were that while aluminum is lighter than steel (fact), the thinner gauge steel only added 15 additional pounds to the deck area (fact), an insignificant .25% (fact), and cut unit costs by $10/corporate costs by $40,000 a year (fact). Clearly, with all facts in place, the VM recommendations were a heavy favorite.

Reasoning and analysis are important to the VM summary, but should only be used to bridge quantitative gaps. Gaping "this, therefore that" holes should be plugged with, "This is how we got here from there." If these holes are not plugged, the whole VM process may be for naught. Managers won't approve what they don't understand, and implementations, not recommendations, are what save the company money.

As in all "sales presentations," the norm of the form is to stress recommendation benefits. For example, what will be improved (costs, quality, productivity, product availability, producibility, maintainability, reliability, life span, etc.)? What will be eliminated (ongoing problems, expensive components, long lead times, high labor costs, etc.)? What benefits can we predict (a greater market share, a captive market via a patentable idea, etc.)?

Franchise Fixtures Incorporated (Manhattan, NY) found that a VM change in packaging would give more protection to the product (slashing a 7% damage rate to zero), cut some packing costs by 60%, and improve productivity in inventory and handling. VM presentations can usually sell via the sizzle (the benefits) and not the steak (specific changes).

Once the VM team has presented what it thinks should be done (the recommendations), the team needs to show management how to do it (suggested implementation).

Recommendations without implementations are fireplaces without heat. *Implemented* ideas save money. The VM team's implementation ideal is to present management decision-makers with a plan of action and a timetable. What needs to be done and when. Who does what and when (this includes both when a person starts and finishes). Who is responsible for what and when. Who supervises who, what and when. When are players ships that pass in the night, when are their actions synchronized, when are they supposed to cross currents? Who, what, when, where, why, how, etc.

Implementation schedules can be presented in memo form, calendar form, or via CPM (Critical Path Method) charts. In either case, the Implementation Phase should be clearly mapped. We want no uncharted waters.

The Recommendation/Implementation Phase is where things either come together or fall apart. "Change" may not be an easy sale, but VM benefits are a best buy. A solid recommendation and implementation presentation can help a VM team and its business backer buy a one-way (onwards and upwards!) ticket to improved corporate competitiveness.

Appendix A

An ounce of application is worth a ton of abstraction (Booker's Law). Ergo, here's a real world VM case study from square one to squared away. The case in point is a Pittsburgh manufacturer.[1]

Here are the basics: "XYZ" company sales representatives submitted price quotations to prospective purchasers in a specially printed (company name, address, logo) three-ring plastic binder. However, salespeople learned that clients were throwing the binders away because they took up too much filing space. Could VM identify a higher-quality product alternative (e.g., one that actually *provided* the necessary product functions) with a lower cost?

Point-blank: how does a corporate component go from *no* good to *so* good?

THE COMMITMENT CAVEAT/SELLING THE VM IDEA

No problem here. For over 20 years, management had demonstrated a commitment to Value Management. The company had a VP for VM. Management stood solidly behind the program and was

---

[1]While the basic facts and study results are real world scores, some of the play-by-play is extrapolation.

up front about its benefits; quoting from one corporate VM brochure, ". . . efforts in the past have enabled [us] to: Invest dollars in many new facilities and more productive facilities. Invest dollars in accelerated new product development. Invest dollars in low prices where necessary to be more competitive." All employees were given publications that explained how VM worked. In short, VM was as ingrained in the corporate culture as were paychecks.

SELECTING THE APPROPRIATE PROJECT

Failing to conduct a VM study on this component would have been a case of Value *Mismanagement*. Prime reason: the binder *did not fulfill its necessary functions* (e.g., clients were not using it, they were throwing it away). No function means no purpose, no purpose means no need for the product. This "means test" proved that a VM study was appropriate. Make that "obligatory."

There were other benefits to studying the too-big binder. Since it was a minor outside purchased (rather than a major in-house manufactured) commodity, product changes would not be terribly traumatic or extremely expensive. Due to the special printing, the product's bottom-line price was out-of-line with standard functional alternatives (specially made products, specially paid prices). The long printing lag/inventory storage time was a long-standing headache. The product had "too" problems: it was too think, too heavy, too complicated, too extravagant. As the product undoubtedly had suitable off-the-rack substitutes, the VM study would not be very long or involved. A high ROI was nigh.

It was clearly possible to spend a buck and save a bundle, to improve a product (e.g., provide necessary functions), and—in short—to become more competitive by simultaneously increasing quality and cutting costs.

SELECTING THE VM TEAM

In this study, the issue was not "who makes the team"; it was "why make a team." Value Management is simple-minded (e.g., why make something more complex than it needs to be?). A low-cost, low-volume product doesn't merit a high-cost, voluminous study. Sometimes it doesn't even merit a team.

Small-scope VM studies are often conducted by a single person. The XYZ study required knowledge from purchasing, sales, and vendor specialists; but all of the necessary information was easily collected via a few well-worded VM inqueries. To put it bluntly, one internal Value specialist worked the works. No band of merry men, just a one-man band.

THE INFORMATION PHASE

By questioning the marketing manager, supply warehouse manager, purchasing manager, and office manager, the Value specialist managed to gather the following relevant information:

- The firm's 1/4"-thick sales quotations (which consisted of a transmittal letter and a few pages of product information) did not require a 1" ring binder. That's a 4:1 space overrun. In addition, the binder was not providing any functions because clients were filing it in the round file. (Source: marketing manager.)

- The three-ring binders cost 79 cents each. They were "anatomically" standard; however, their promotional printing made them a special order item requiring minimum purchase lots of 5,000. The company used approximately 4,000 units per year. (Source: supply warehouse manager.)

- Numerous vendors provided the same product to the company at a comparable cost. All had comparable purchasing conditions. (Source: purchasing department.)

- Since quotation materials had to be punched and individually assembled, they were sometimes held up in the secretarial section until someone had time to prepare them. (Source: office manager.)

THE FUNCTION PHASE

Together, the Value specialist and marketing manager identified the binder's two necessary product functions:

1. To protect the enclosed material (physically protect the pages and visually protect privileged information from curious competitors). Protect material.

2. To identify the enclosed material ("This quotation is brought to you by . . . ."). Identify material.

The two professionals agreed that "protect material" was the primary function. "Identify material" was a secondary—albeit important—concern. Any alternative binding system would, as a minimum, have to provide these two functions.

THE CREATIVE PHASE

At this point, the study turned into a vendor enlisted, vendor assisted project. With help from the purchasing department, the Value specialist identified current office product vendors and prospective purveyors. All were given the following basic VM guidelines and important VM information:

> The XYZ Company is soliciting creative ideas from vendors.
>
> Our sales quotes are printed on $8^1/2''$ by $11''$ paper and consist of no more than four pages (a letter of transmittal and product literature). They are bound in standard three-ring binders with $1''$ rings. The binders are specialty printed with promotional information (company name, address, logo). The binders cost 79 cents each and the minimum order lot is 5,000 (annual use: 4,000 units).
>
> We recently learned that clients are throwing away the binders because they are too bulky. We wish to purchase an alternative product(s)/system(s) that—at the minimum—provides two specific functions:
>
> 1. Protects the enclosed material (physically protects the pages and visually protects privileged information from curious competitors).
> 2. Identifies the enclosed material (a promotional function).
>
> There are absolutely no constraints on the product beyond the necessity of providing these functions. Systems that do not require costly specialty printing or hole-punching would be a benefit.
>
> We'd like your input. Do you sell, or can you devise, any alternative system(s) that will meet our functional requirements? What are their advantages? At what cost and under what purchasing conditions? Etc. (Reference attached forms.)
>
> A purchasing decision will be made within four weeks. XYZ agrees to purchase the chosen product from the proposing

vendor for a minimum period of two years (given that the product price does not increase by more than 10%). We hope to hear from you soon.

Sincerely,

THE EVALUATION PHASE

Five vendors accepted the competitive challenge. Using VM directions, they refined and combined their current products (on such a small-scale project, no VMer would expect a total product redesign) and provided costs for five appropriate functional alternatives:

Vendor A—Smaller three-ring binder, 3/4″ rings, with specialty printing
  Unit cost 63 cents
  Start-up cost of minimum purchase: $3,150 for 5,000 units
  1 1/3-year supply

Vendor B—Thin-comb binding with specialty printed paper covers
  Unit cost 29 cents
  Start-up cost of $750 for comb-hole puncher, approximately $35 for supply of combs, $25 for cover printing, $200 for cover design
  3-month supply

Vendor C—Manila envelope with personalized labels
  Unit cost 11 cents
  Start-up cost of $35 for labels, envelopes already in stock
  6-month supply

Vendor D—File folder with metal clamp and rubber stamped company name/address/logo
  Unit cost 14 cents
  Start-up cost of $40 for large rubber stamp, files/clamps/stamp pad already in stock
  Length of supply N/A

Vendor E—Clear plastic sheets with a snap-on spine
  Unit cost 13 cents
  No start-up cost other than initial purchase
  Length of supply N/A

The Value specialist conducted an evaluation by comparison. A short summary:

Vendor A—Smaller three-ring binder, 3/4" rings, specialty printing

Advantages: less likely to be thrown away by customers, less expensive than the current alternative, professional looking, not a major change.

Disadvantages: has most of the disadvantages of its big brother (the cost of specialty printing, 5,000 unit minimum order, inventory storage, hole punching, etc.). Major concern—a 3/4" binder may not be small enough to meet client's needs.

Since Alternative A might not have met functional requirements (e.g., it can't protect or identify materials if clients throw it away), the product was dropped from further consideration.

Vendor B—Thin comb-binding, specialty printed covers

Advantages: fulfills product functions, available from many vendors, comb sizes (10 available) are easily matched to quotation thickness, professional appearance, specialty printing would be done on heavy paper (less expensive than printing on binders), maximum flexibility on promotional designs, minimum quantity purchase insignificant, variable size combs could be used on other company publications.

Disadvantages: high start-up cost, additional overhead and puncher storage required, page changes are relatively difficult, greater probability of binding error, comb-bound publications can be difficult to read if wrong comb sizes are selected.

Vendor C—Manila envelope with personalized company labels

Advantages: inexpensive (envelopes vs. binders and printing labels vs. printing binders), already in common use around the office, minimal overhead, no punching costs, universal product availability, no minimum order on envelopes.

Disadvantages: major concern—may not meet the product function "protect material." The material has to be removed from the envelope to use it. There it is—defenseless. The $64,000 question: will the buyer put the material *back* in the manila envelope? This is not SOP for most materials—e.g., mail—that come in envelopes. Customer custom would have to change, but buyer behavior is not within the jurisdiction of the seller.

Since Alternative B might not have met functional requirements, the product was dropped from further consideration.

Vendor D—File folder with metal clamp and rubber stamped company name/address/logo

Advantages: less likely to be thrown away than original binder (indeed, it should be ideal for client filing systems), relatively inexpensive, universally available, no minimum order, already in use around the office.

Disadvantages: major concern—may not effectively meet the product function "identify material." This is defensive divining. The file folder may be too similar to the buyer's in-house filing system (ergo, easily mislaid, misrouted, misfiled, etc., in non-vendor material). A mistaken identity could result in missed sales.

Since Alternative D might not have met functional requirements, the product was dropped from further consideration.

Vendor E—Clear plastic sheets with a snap-on spine

Advantages: provides primary product function, less likely to be thrown away than original binder, minimal overhead (the clamp-on spine eliminates punching costs, etc.), universal product availability, easy assembly and easy page changes, no minimum order.

Disadvantages: major concern—could not be specialty printed. However . . .

When the transmittal letter (printed on corporate letterhead) was placed immediately inside the clear plastic cover, it shielded inside information (protected material) and promoted the company (identified material via letterhead). Ergo, the disadvantage could be diffused.

Conclusion: three viable alternatives were identified. Weighing the advantages and disadvantages of each suggested that the best option might be the clear plastic sheets with a snap-on spine.

THE INVESTIGATION PHASE

A study of this magnitude (well, mini-tude) does not necessitate additional consultations with specialists, manufacturers, etc. To determine if Alternative E met functional needs, the Value specialist simply showed it to the marketing manager, sales personnel, office personnel, buyers, etc., to solicit negative feedback. When there was none, he knew he'd found a plastic pièce de résistance.

THE RECOMMENDATION PHASE

Because the marketing manager (who had the power to accept or reject recommendations) was aware of the project problem, had participated in the study, and had already given his feedback, the final acceptance of Alternative E was almost assured.

However, a smart value specialist doesn't take acceptance for granted. This one certainly didn't. He gave the marketing manager a synopsis of past problems, current possibilities, and future benefits. Then he asked for a timely decision (one week) to be followed by immediate recommendation implementation (e.g., marketing manager to inform the purchasing manager that as of X date, binders would be replaced with the clear plastic product, to be purchased from Vendor E for no less than two years at a unit price not to exceed 14.3 cents). The recommendation was accepted and implemented post haste.

Appendix B

As the old saying goes, "You can't buy health." Today that's not the half, or even the quarter, of it. The current cliché is more along the line of "You can't buy health—and even if you could, you couldn't afford it."

America's health care system is living proof that opposites attract. Rising medical costs attract lower payment percentages from budget-blinded government programs (Medicaid, Medicare . . . Medican't) and cost-conscious private insurers (some cynics have gone so far as to suggest renaming Blue Cross "Blue Crossout"). Rising public expectations, such as longer life span and miracle cures (e.g. thinner thighs in 30 days without even buying a bestseller!), are coupled with a rising indignation at health care costs. Today's expensive medical insurance deductibles are as high as yesterday's inexpensive operations. Patients could theoretically recover from minor surgery, only to suffer a major coronary when confronted with their bill.

Fortunately, there is a light at the end of the tunnel for the enlightened. As the 98 member hospitals of the Hospital Council of Western Pennsylvania (and associated hospitals in Maryland and New York) learned, Value Management can help hospitals sever unnecessary costs.[1]

---

[1]While the basic facts and study results are real world scores, some of the play-by-play is extrapolation.

Want to know how they trimmed the fat? Suture self and read on.

THE BASICS

Like most hospitals, members of the Western Pennsylvania Co-op gave all incoming patients a standard admissions kit. In this Council's case, the standard kit contained 57 different personal care items. Were these expensive items necessities or niceties? A VM team decided to find out.

THE COMMITMENT CAVEAT/SELLING THE VM IDEA

Just as it isn't hard to sell a product or service that people want to buy, it isn't difficult to sell staff members on an idea that will make their job burden a little lighter load.

Rising health care costs affect all industry insiders, hitting everybody from the operating room to the boiler room. But concurrent cuts in insurance benefits and hospital revenues (due to uncollectible accounts, higher insurance copayments, reduced government payments, etc.) cut hospital helpers both ways.

Here's how. Hospital staff pay insurance premiums, deductibles, etc., just like the rest of us (there's no such thing as a free lunch, even when you are the one doing the cooking). They too, are victims of premium-price premiums.

Meanwhile, as hospital revenues work their way down, workers find themselves down and out. Raises aren't. Employees are let go. Cost of living increases (actually "hold your owns") and/or training programs and/or quality care let up. Soon, working at the institution is a real let down.

In short, hospital employees are paying more for what they get, and getting less for what they do. It's not robbing Peter to pay Paul. It's both disciples being held hostage for a Profit.

Enter Value Management and its high-quality, low-cost commitment. Of course the hospital staff "should be committed"—and it is. It is survival of the fiscally fittest. (NOTE: The 98 member council is so committed to Value Management that it has a CVS on staff full time). Commitment is what makes Value Management work. For workers—and for management.

SELECTING THE APPROPRIATE PROJECT

It was clear from the start that startling savings would accrue from the admissions kit study.[2] Simply asking the "acid tests" of value was enough to give testy team members acid indigestion. For example:

- Does every function/component of the product/system process in question add value?

    The answer was no. Team members were aware that many of the items were routinely tossed or lost—at great cost.

- Is the value of the function/component in line with its cost?

    Again, the answer was no. Several admissions kit items performed two-bit functions at a bit higher cost. In short, they bit off less than they could chew.

- Does the product/system require all of its components/functions?

    Yet another no. In fact, the team not only found kit items that performed unnecessary functions—two of these ghastly goods were actually detrimental to patient health!

- Can a standard part, or other substitute, replace a more expensive unit? Or, along the same vein, can a service be supplied via a less expensive process? Are you providing a low-volume product through expensive high-volume methods (or vice versa)?

    The answers were an unequivocal yes, a meaningful maybe, and a definite "it depends." Using a function focus, staff members quickly identified items that had fourteen-carat costs, yet delivered only a penny's worth of performance. At least nine components had a caviar cost structure while providing only fish-egg functions. Something was fishy.

    Even without these acid tests of value, there were other indications that the study would be a sulfuric success. The project met many general project selection criteria:

---

[2]Other VM studies were conducted by the team with equal success. For example, a study performed on urinary catheter care saved the Council over $1.3 million annually.

- the subject was relatively complex (e.g., the admissions kit contained 57 different components)
- the items were easy to define and understand relative to their functions/objectives (e.g., everybody knows what slippers, toothpaste, pencils, etc., are supposed to do)
- the admissions kits were easily changed (e.g., since components were separate items simply packaged together for convenience, dropping individual items was no packaging pain)
- the kit was too much of a good thing (e.g., it contained items that many—and in some cases, most!—patients never used)
- the kit was. under the control of the hospital (e.g., it contained items specifically requested by the facility).

In summary, a few cursory questions suggested that the admissions kit was long on unnecessary products and short on cost efficiency. That was the long and short of it.

SELECTING THE VM TEAM

Years ago, Andrew Carnegie tried to interest George M. Pullman in a joint venture: building railroad sleeping cars. Pullman turned a deaf ear—until he heard Carnegie's proposed name for the cooperative carriages. As you may have guessed, Carnegie didn't want to call them "Pullman cars" because they pulled sleeping men around the country. The name, according to Pullman, "had a real ring to it."

Carnegie's true genius was in understanding people. Carnegie knew that Pullman would be more likely to jump into the joint venture if he felt that he had some ownership in the idea. That premise is also practiced in MBO (e.g., Management By Objective, where the employee sets his own objectives and is judged by his ability to meet them), QC (Quality Circles, which lead to "joint ownership" of ideas), and ETC (Every Theory Current). It doesn't take a PhD to figure out why.

Innovative ownership is a theory critical to (not critical of!) VM team selection. In the admissions kit case, team members were chosen because:

- they had knowledge necessary to the project
   The various knowledge bases represented were administrative, medical, logistics, inventory control, etc.

and because

- they represented groups that would be directly affected by any proposed changes

The team members were as follows:

- two nurses
- one pharmacist
- one management engineer
- director of housekeeping
- central supply supervisor
- materials manager

NOTE: The specialty closest to patient care, nursing, was represented by two team members. This proves VM's commitment to quality (e.g., a less expensive admissions kit must not lead to a cheapening of patient care).

It was important that all facility factions be represented. A decision can't be all for one and one for all unless all are represented, one way or another. A good VM project, like the U.S. government, is run BY the people and FOR the people—not TO the people.

THE INFORMATION PHASE

The 57 personal care items involved were reminiscent of Heinz 57 Sauce—lots of individual goodies adding spice to the total package.

However, in the case of the admissions kit, too many cooks had spoiled the broth. Numerous expensive items—some of which were doubtless unnecessary—had been added to the kit's routine recipe. Among the items studied—and eventually found wanting/unwanted—were:

- mouthwashes
- soap
- bath oil
- toothbrush holder
- towelettes
- toothpaste
- denture cup
- slippers

- oral swabs
- sanitary napkin
- pencil
- lemon glycerine swabs
- disposable washclothes
- body lotions
- body powder

The VM team asked basic questions about each item, for example:

- What was the original need for the product? Have the original needs changed? Why, and to what?
- What changes were considered when the new needs were identified? Why was this option chosen?
- Does this solution to the needs issue involve any special problems? Particular opportunities?
- Does this item meet any particular requirements (standards imposed by outside medical authorities, for example)?
- How is the product used (how many are used, how often, in what quantities, etc.)?
- Why is the product used?
- Are these products currently being improved/modified?
- What areas have the greatest potential for cost/quality/usage improvement?
- Are there any constraints/requirements/preferences regarding size, functionality, life span (for example, disposable vs. reusable), operability, design options, environmental hazards/conditions (past, present, or future)?
- What is the product's documented history in terms of:
  a) safety record
  b) key components
  c) complaint/compliment feedback from patients
  d) complaint/compliment feedback from staff
  e) defect rate
  f) nonusage
  g) refills for patients

- What do other hospitals, medical professionals, recognized authorities, staff, etc. recommend and/or use themselves?
- Can a different but similar item offer more value?
- Is the admissions kit the most effective distribution system for this item?
- What is the cost of each item? The cost of providing each item?
- Are we specifying the most appropriate item (brand, manufacturer, size, shape, usability, etc.)?
- Can we substitute a standard item for a special issue?
- If these items are not all being used, why?

These were not the end all of the information phase. They were just the begin all. The team had to ask VM questions about these VM answers. For example:

- Where can we get additional information?
- Can anyone deny or verify what we think we've learned via the initial questions?
- Can anyone offer ancillary information that might be of value?[3]

Clearly, gathering the data was no mean feat. It took a lot of fancy footwork. That's why the Information Phase is truly the time that tries men's soles!

THE FUNCTION PHASE

The team was able to make much of this long story short by using an abridged version of the old VM Q&A.[4] Its first-run, "Cliff's Notes" condensation consisted of a single question: does this product provide a necessary function?

---

[3]Multiply these questions by 57 and it's easy to see how an over anxious VM team could suffer from overview overload. To quote one well known CVS, "Don't bite off more than you can chew—unless you intend to choke on it."

[4]None of the items were expensive enough, or important enough, to warrant extended analysis. Besides, as the team had suspected, their elementary examination would identify significant savings.

Interestingly, several products did not and were immediately eliminated from the admissions kit caper.[5] For example:

- Mouthwash was identified as a "medicated liquid used to cleanse the mouth" and "for treating diseased states of the oral mucous membrane" (generating "kiss-blow-zzzzing sex appeal!" was not considered a valid function).

During preliminary research, team members found that the Council on Dental Therapeutics' (CDT) did not recognize any medicinal value to the "unsupervised use of mouthwashes by the general public."

Therefore, the general and uncontrolled distribution of mouthwashes via the standard admissions kit was discontinued (NOTE: However, as per CDT recommendations, therapeutic mouthwashes would be prescribed by doctors and controlled by staff pharmacists).

By going "straight to the horses mouth," VM team members were able to cut straight to the bottom line—and cut out an unnecessary expense.

Not only was body powder found to be void of necessary functions (despite its comforting characteristics and popularity with patients), VM team members felt that it should be avoided for health reasons.

Research found the commercial talcum powder (a combination of talc—hydrous magnesium silicate—and other silicates) has been linked to pneumoconiosis, lung cancer, cancer of the pleura, vaginal irritation, cancer of the gastrointestinal tract, infantile powder aspiration (sometimes leading to severe bronchiolear obstruction, respiratory distress, and death), etc.

These links identify body powder as a weak link in the hospital chain. Spilled powder also presented a danger to convalescent constitutionals. In short, this admissions kit item was hazardous to patient health. Body powders took a powder during the review—never to return to the kit and kaboodle.

(NOTE: Some people are drawn to corn starch, a potential substitute for body powder which has its own drawbacks. Because

---

[5]Many of the "unnecessary" products were still made available to patients upon request. However, many of the items (body lotion and bath oil, for example) were dispensed in smaller bottles. Large economy size servings were replaced with items sized to the average patient stay (seven days).

the medium is a good media for bacterial growth, and in fact has many of talc's unpleasant properties, it did not replace body powder in the admissions kit).

- Bath oil—while serving a valuable function as a skin moisturizer—was also found to have all the *medicinal* merit of snake oil. In addition, VMers found that it presented a health hazard (slippage in the bathtub). Bath oil was subsequently drilled from the admissions kit.

- Body lotions—which were used to comfort/moisturize suffering skin and reduce unsanitary smells—were found to be a functional frill. A big pay out with no corollary payback.

The remaining subjects were subjected to further, more formal, functional analysis (as outlined in the Creative Phase/Evaluation Phase).

THE CREATIVE PHASE/THE EVALUATION PHASE[6]

VM team members found several other items which performed menial functions better provided through other means. For example:

- The primary functions of oral swabs—to freshen a patient's breath and loosen large pieces of dental debris—were better met through the use of a tongue blade wrapped in gauze. Better results, better price—you'd better believe the VM team was sold on this substitution!

- Disposable towelettes and disposable washcloths—used for patient cleansing—were replaced by reusable washclothes. Why? Better functional fulfillment. The "real" thing offered more friction, did not clog up facility plumbing, and was already being used in other hospital areas. That made "real" washclothes a really good deal.

- Toothbrush holders—function: to separate toothbrush from sink surface—were replaced by paper towels. This is the perfect example of a functional (and financial) favorite forcing out the fanciful!

---

[6]In small studies like this, it can be difficult to determine when one phase is phased in, and another is phased out. So don't allow yourself to get phased!

When it came to items that provided necessary functions, the creative consensus was to provide a week's worth of each wonder ware, rather than a lavish level for a lifetime. These products included:

- Toothpaste (team members also decided that the additional cost for fluoridated fabrications was not justified, given the average patient's short seven day stay)
- Soap (1 1/2 ounces was enough for average patient practices)

After functional analysis, the remaining items—lemon glycerine swabs, slippers, pencils, facial tissues, denture cups, sanitary napkins, etc.—were found to have measurable merit. But . . . asked the creative council . . . did the distribution system, the admissions kit itself? Should the kit itself be discontinued? It was a high-quality question. Consider the following phenomena:

- Lemon glycerine swabs were typically used by postoperative and/or elderly patients who had difficulty taking their fluids orally. Translation: they were only needed by an unfortunate few.
- Denture cups, though valuable to some patients, were valueless to others. Why indenture the budget over this low use luxury? Why not simply give cups to the "needy"?
- Bringing slippers to the hospital may slip some patients' minds, but many people preferred to furnish their own favored footwear. Why slip them an unnecessary—and costly—pair?
- It's a fact that sanitary napkins were only needed by a paltry percentage of the facility's female faction (tampons were eliminated as both a standard supply and on-request item because of their connection to toxic shock syndrome).
- Pencils could be distributed to patients during their initial interview with the dietician. This distribution system had the added benefit of client contact/communication.

In short, this creative "ask task" helped the VM team go beyond it original study parameters—into a paradise of potential savings.

THE INVESTIGATION PHASE

In the Investigation Phase, the VM team utilized a concept popular with medical professionals: the second opinion. Team members discussed admissions kits needs with other medical professionals, valued vendors, recognized health care authorities, and member facilities. Their informational archaeology dug up some interesting facts:

- Of the 57 standard admissions kit items, only six were used by all patients. Translation: the facility was funding 51 functional faux pas.

- All of the six common-use components were available through other distribution channels (via standard supply areas, nurses stations, the housekeeping system, etc.). It didn't take double vision to see the duplicated costs.

- Many hospital staff members cannibalized complete sets for single items, incapacitating the costly kits. It was a high-cost handicap.

- The simple existence of the admissions kit encouraged employees to suggest other expensive, but not necessarily needed, items. And who has the temperate temperament to avoid such a temptation?

The study specifics lead to a low-cost conclusion. Go with the factual flow and dam the admissions kit. Sink the sucker, full steam ahead.

THE RECOMMENDATION PHASE

It's always good to have a full head of steam going into the Recommendation Phase. Often, managers resist giving euthanasia to a pet project, even when it's a monkey on everybody's back. Ongoing opponents to change rally against the VM cause just because. Vendors vie to keep profit-packed programs. Change can be a hard sell; it has to be done one cell at a time.

However, in this case, the hard sell gave way to soft soap. The seeds of success had been planted early, thanks to "sow and tell." Departments affected by the change (nursing, pharmacy, house-

keeping, etc.) had all had a hand in handing in the recommendations. Since inside experts and outside authorities had been asked
for input, they felt consulted—not insulted. Thus, profitable planning resulted in general support for the kit's elimination.

NOTE: Any risks involved in eliminating the health care kit
were small. Dunning demands for its return could realistically
result in the product's insurrection resurrection. No big deal. So
thanks to VM, the unnecessary kit was declared DOA—Doomed
On Advice.

Appendix C

Value Program Survey

Sometimes it helps to get a testimonial straight from the horse's mouth, undistorted by any back-of-the animal anatomy.

The Society of American Value Engineers recently conducted a Value Program Survey of corporate members to gauge the success of their internal, ongoing programs (see Value Management figure). Respondents included Allied Automotive (Bendix Heavy Vehicles Systems Division), Allis-Chalmers Corporation, Brunswick Corporation, Chamberlain Consumer Products Groups (Electronics Division), Cleveland Pneumatic Company, The Foxboro Company, Freightliner Corporation, Holmes and Marver Inc., Honeywell Inc., (Defense Systems Division), Hughes Aircraft Company, IBM, Ingersoll Rand Co., J.I. Case Co. (Worldwide Agricultural Engineering), John Deere Harvestor Works, Joy Manufacturing Company, Martin Marietta Orlando Aerospace, Parker Hannifin Corporation (Aerospace Hydraulics Branch), Tenneco—J.I. Case, Westinghouse Electronic Corporation, etc. Read it straight from the horse's mouth—you'll see why CVSs are nags when it comes to the continuing use of Value Management.

RESPONSE TO VALUE PROGRAM SURVEY

GENERAL INFORMATION

COMPANY NAME: Allis-Chalmers Corporation

ADDRESS: Box 512, Milwaukee, Wisconsin 53201

PRODUCTS OR SERVICES PROVIDED:

Agricultural tractors and combines, bulk material handling, solid and mineral processing (crushers, screens, cement plants), fluid processing (pumps, hydro-turbines, compressors), coal gas plants.

ORGANIZATION OF VALUE PROGRAM

COMPANY DOES HAVE A CONTINUING VALUE PROGRAM

PROGRAM DOES EMPLOY FORMAL WORKSHOPS AS A ROUTINE ELEMENT

VALUE PROGRAM REPORTS TO:

Associate Director, Manufacturing and Computer Applications Technology, Advanced Technology Center

VALUE PROGRAM IS APPLIED IN THE FOLLOWING AREAS:

Product design, overhead accounts, manufacturing processes

PERFORMANCE OF VALUE PROGRAM

ANNUAL VALUE PROGRAM EXPENDITURE: $100,000

PROFITABILITY ENHANCEMENT DUE TO VALUE PROGRAM:

Total dollar amount $6.9 million per year (over last two years)

0.5% of net sales

VALUE PROGRAM HAS ENHANCED MARKET POSITION AS FOLLOWS:

We don't have proof positive that it has. However, products Value Analyzed are less costly to produce and more reliable. Also we have greater quality.

OTHER BENEFITS ACHIEVED:

Develops personal and leadership qualities in personnel, builds organizational teamwork, improves interdepartmental communications, increases productivity, teaches personnel to be more creative in other work situations.

FOR MORE DETAILED INFORMATION CONCERNING VALUE PROGRAM CONTACT:

A. L. Cnilstrom
Manager, Tech-Based Cost Improvement
c/o Advanced Technology Center
Allis-Chalmers Corporation
Milwaukee, Wisconsin 53201

EXAMPLES OF VALUE STUDIES AND THE BENEFITS ACHIEVED:

Before Value Engineering, our holdback line was too costly to produce and still be competitive. After VE, a more versatile design halved its weight, tripled its maximum capacity, increased its models from five to 12, all while reducing product costs by 28%.

Note: Since this survey was taken, Allis-Chalmers has fallen on the hard times. To restate a statute: VM can resusitate, but it can't resurrect.

RESPONSE TO VALUE PROGRAM SURVEY

GENERAL INFORMATION

COMPANY NAME: Cleveland Pneumatic Company

ADDRESS: 3871 East 77th St., Cleveland, OH 44105

PRODUCTS OF SERVICES PROVIDED:

Design and manufacturer of aircraft landing gear

ORGANIZATION OF VALUE PROGRAM

COMPANY DOES HAVE A CONTINUING VALUE PROGRAM

PROGRAM DOES EMPLOY FORMAL WORKSHOPS AS A ROUTINE ELEMENT

VALUE PROGRAM REPORTS TO:

Director, Advanced Engineering, responsible for engineering design development and conceptual designs for new gears

VALUE PROGRAM IS APPLIED IN THE FOLLOWING AREAS:

Product design, manufacturing process

PERFORMANCE OF VALUE PROGRAM

ANNUAL VALUE PROGRAM EXPENDITURE: $100,000

PROFITABILITY ENHANCEMENT DUE TO VALUE PROGRAM:

Total dollar amount $750,000

0.4% of net sales

VALUE PROGRAM HAS ENHANCED MARKET POSITION AS FOLLOWS:

Customer goodwill is enhanced. We are the major company in our industry and the customers (and Department of Defense) like to know we have an ongoing effort to reduce cost [and improve quality].

OTHER BENEFITS ACHIEVED:

Other team members experience personal growth. Long lasting benefits include improved communications across organizational lines and the feeling that an individual can influence the organization. Also cross-pollinization of knowledge, ideas and feelings occur.

FOR MORE DETAILED INFORMATION CONCERNING
VALUE PROGRAM CONTACT:

Howard Eckstein, CVS
Value Engineer
Cleveland Pneumatic Company
3871 East 77th St.
Cleveland, OH 44105

EXAMPLES OF VALUE STUDIES AND THE BENEFITS
ACHIEVED:

none released

RESPONSE TO VALUE PROGRAM SURVEY

GENERAL INFORMATION

COMPANY NAME: The Foxboro Company

ADDRESS: Neponset Ave., Foxboro, MA 02035

PRODUCTS OR SERVICES PROVIDED:

Process instruments and broad computer-based systems for process management and control.

ORGANIZATION OF VALUE PROGRAM

COMPANY DOES HAVE A CONTINUING VALUE PROGRAM

PROGRAM DOES EMPLOY FORMAL WORKSHOPS AS A ROUTINE ELEMENT

VALUE PROGRAM REPORTS TO:

Manager of Internal Training

VALUE PROGRAM IS APPLIED IN THE FOLLOWING AREAS:

Training. Our approach is to provide training to all disciplines. The purpose of this approach is to inculcate the Value Engineering methodology in our people. They in turn, armed with the techniques, integrate them in their daily routine. The measurement of improvements is the responsibility of line managers and supervisors. In other words, we do not have a separate, competing, group analyzing other designs or service functions. We operate under the philosophy, ''Feed a man a fish and you feed him for a day. Teach him to fish and you feed him for a lifetime.''

PERFORMANCE OF VALUE PROGRAM

ANNUAL VALUE PROGRAM EXPENDITURE:

not released

PROFITABILITY ENHANCEMENT DUE TO VALUE PROGRAM:

not released

VALUE PROGRAM HAS ENHANCED MARKET POSITION AS FOLLOWS:

not released

OTHER BENEFITS ACHIEVED:

Benefits are achieved by improving the value of our people via training. They in turn improve the value of our products and services by using the value techniques. There is no central measuring system; it is done by line managers/supervisors.

FOR MORE DETAILED INFORMATION CONCERNING VALUE PROGRAM CONTACT:

William S. Santos
Principal Instructor
The Foxboro Company
Bristol Park Education Center
Foxboro, MA 02035

EXAMPLES OF VALUE STUDIES AND THE BENEFITS ACHIEVED:

not released

RESPONSE TO VALUE PROGRAM SURVEY

GENERAL INFORMATION

COMPANY NAME: Hughes Aircraft Company

ADDRESS: PO Box 1042, El Segundo, CA 90245

PRODUCTS OR SERVICES PROVIDED:

The Company's capability is in the advanced electronics based on a history of technological first in space and communications, missiles and avionics, air defense, command and control, industrial electronics and basic research.

ORGANIZATION OF VALUE PROGRAM

COMPANY DOES HAVE A CONTINUING VALUE PROGRAM

PROGRAM DOES EMPLOY FORMAL WORKSHOPS AS A ROUTINE ELEMENT

VALUE PROGRAM REPORTS TO:

Director of Product Cost Effectiveness

VALUE PROGRAM IS APPLIED IN THE FOLLOWING AREAS:

Product design, information systems, manufacturing processes, service activities

PERFORMANCE OF VALUE PROGRAM

ANNUAL VALUE PROGRAM EXPENDITURES:

over $11 million

PROFITABILITY ENHANCEMENT DUE TO VALUE PROGRAM:

Total dollar amount: $611 million in total negotiated savings since 1964.

3% of net sales

VALUE PROGRAM HAS ENHANCED MARKET POSITION AS FOLLOWS:

Expands market potential. Enhances competitive position. Allows for the incorporation of new technology. Provides increase in produce capability. Reduces contract cost commitments and previous funds for needed change. Keeps the program sold.

OTHER BENEFITS ACHIEVED:

Deters unnecessary/costly requirements. Reduces over-runs. Improves cash flow. Increases earnings on current and follow-up contracts. Reduces or eliminates non-cost effective requirements.

FOR MORE DETAILED INFORMATION CONCERNING VALUE PROGRAM CONTACT:

W. H. Cooperman, CVS
Manager VE
Hughes Aircraft Company
PO Box 1042
Building C2 M/S 189
El Segundo, CA 90245

EXAMPLES OF VALUE STUDIES AND THE BENEFITS ACHIEVED:

A U.S. Navy contract for standard data display systems improved design and manufacturing techniques and saved over $40 million over production quantities.

RESPONSE TO VALUE PROGRAM SURVEY

GENERAL INFORMATION

COMPANY NAME: IBM

ADDRESS: FSD Owego, Owego, NY 13827

PRODUCTS OR SERVICES PROVIDED:

Computer systems for military and space programs

ORGANIZATION OF VALUE PROGRAM

COMPANY DOES HAVE A CONTINUING VALUE PROGRAM

PROGRAM DOES EMPLOY FORMAL WORKSHOPS AS A ROUTINE ELEMENT

VALUE PROGRAM REPORTS TO:

Industrial Engineering

VALUE PROGRAM IS APPLIED IN THE FOLLOWING AREAS:

Product design, manufacturing processes, service activities

PERFORMANCE OF VALUE PROGRAM

ANNUAL VALUE PROGRAM EXPENDITURE:

not released

PROFITABILITY ENHANCEMENT DUE TO VALUE PROGRAM:

Total dollar amount $43 million annually

5% of net sales

VALUE PROGRAM HAS ENHANCED MARKET POSITION AS FOLLOWS:

Has been used on proposals to drive costs down to targets

OTHER BENEFITS ACHIEVED:

VECPS (Value Engineering Change Proposals)—which are added profit—$1.6 million in one year. Development of cost consciousness and capability to apply VE concepts.

FOR MORE DETAILED INFORMATION CONCERNING VALUE PROGRAM CONTACT:

A. F. Kaufmann 0114
Manager, Value Engineering
IBM FSD
Owego, NY 13827

EXAMPLES OF VALUE STUDIES AND THE BENEFITS ACHIEVED:
not released

Final Note

Claiming to completely cover the subject of VM on the preceding pages would be like teaching brain surgery via 25 words or less: cut open, fix up, sew together, bill patient. In VM, there's no substitute for formal training and on-the-job experience. To cut all unnecessary costs and to avoid any scars on a product or service's reputation for quality, it is important that studies be led by a specialist who knows how Value techniques operate.[1]

The designation Certified Value Specialist (CVS) is an accreditation earned through the Society of American Value Engineers. It is not a legal designation like CPA or MD. Therefore, finding a truly competent Value practitioner for a specific project can be difficult. However, a reader can contact SAVERS, the free referral service that matches specific industries/needs/project types/etc. to qualified Value specialists. The address is:

SAVERS (Specialized and Accredited Value Engineers
    Referral Service)
3504 Turner Road S.E.
Salem, OR 97302

---

[1]Companies will eventually develop their own specialists. First time and/or intricate studies, however, should be led by a leader—not a learner.

Bibliography

Selling Dynamics. Allen, Robert Y. and Spohn, Robert F. 512 pages. McGraw-Hill Inc.: 1984.

How to Sell Well: The Art and Science of Professional Salesmanship. McGraw-Hill Inc.: 1971.

High Impact Selling: Power Strategies for Successful Selling. Brooks, William T. Prentice-Hall Inc.: 1988.

You'll Never Get No for an Answer: Positional Selling. Carew, Jack. 240 pages. Simon and Schuster, Inc.: 1987.

The Winning Edge in Selling: Successful Techniques that Tip the Balance. Eastman, Robert E. 208 pages. Prentice-Hall Inc.: 1983.

Confident Selling. Fisher, James R. Prentice-Hall Inc.: 1971.

ABC's of Selling. Futrell, Charles. Richard D. Irwin Inc.: 1988.

Fundamentals of Selling. Futrell, Charles. Richard D. Irwin Inc.: 1988.

How to Sell Anything to Anybody. Girard, Joe and Brown, Stanley H. 240 pages. Warner Books Inc.: 1979.

Selling Skills for the Non-Salesperson: For People Who Hate to Sell but Love to Succeed. Goodman, Gary S. 144 pages. Prentice-Hall Inc.: 1984.

Principles of Creative Selling. Haas, Kenneth B. and Ernest, John. Macmillan Publishing Co.: 1978.

Creative Selling Today. Kossen, Stan. 296 pages. Harper and Row, Publishers Inc.: 1988.

Selling to a Group: Presentation Strategies. LeRoux, Paul. 176 pages. Harper and Row, Publishers Inc.: 1984.

Conceptual Selling. Miller, Robert B. 320 pages. Warner Books Inc.: 1989.

Strategic Selling. Miller, Robert B. 320 pages. Warner Books Inc.: 1989.

Selling—the How and Why: A Comprehensive Introduction to Salesmanship. Norris, James S. 204 pages. Prentice-Hall Inc.: 1982.

Back to Basic Selling. Taylor, Robert F. 240 pages. Prentice-Hall Inc.: 1985.

Sizzlemanship. Wheeler, Elmer. 294 pages. Prentice-Hall Inc.: 1984.

The Ideal Problem Solver: A Guide to Improving Thinking, Learning, and Creativity. Bransford, John D. and Stein, Barry S. 150 pages. W. H. Freeman and Co. Publishers: 1989.

Creativity is Forever. Davis, Gary A. 256 pages. Kendall/Hunt Publishing Co.: 1987.

Personal Productivity through Personal Living. Evans, J. Robert. 192 pages. Kendall/Hunt Publishing Co.: 1981.

The Creative Mind. Findlay, C. Scott and Lumsden, Charles H. 189 pages. The Academic Press: 1988.

Creativity in Business. Crisp, Michael G. 96 pages. Crisp Publications Inc.: 1989.

Creativity and Work. Jaques, Elliott. 237 pages. International Universities Press Inc.: 1989.

The Creative Edge: How to Foster Innovation Where You Work. Miller, William C. 192 pages. Addison-Wesley Publishing Co. Inc.: 1986.

Your Creative Power. Osborn, Alex F. The Scribner Book Companies, Inc.: 1972.

New Directions in Creativity. Mark I. Renzulli, J. S. Creative Learning Press Inc.: 1986.

Increasing Employee Productivity. Tylczak, Lynn. 72 pages. Crisp Publications, Inc.: 1990.

Creative People at Work: Eleven Cognitive Case Studies. Wallace, Doris B. and Gruber, Howard E. 288 pages. Oxford University Press Inc.: 1989.

Twenty Ways to be More Creative in Your Job. Weinstin, Bob. Simon and Schuster, Inc.: 1983.

Unleashing the Right Side of the Brain: The LARC Creativity Program. The Stephen Greene Press: 1987.

Index